Learning C Programming

An Informative and In-depth Guide to C Programming

By

Anthony Wallit

information is without a contract or any type of guaranteed assurance.

The trademarks that are used are without any consent, and the publication of the trademark is without permission or backing by the trademark owner. All trademarks and brands within this book are for clarifying purposes only and are owned by the owners themselves, not affiliated with this document.

Contents

Introduction

C is a simple and basic programming language to learn. This book covers the fundamentals of C, as well as the C Basic Library and current C standards. It is not necessary to have any prior programming expertise.

C is a popular programming language that has been popular for decades. C has a wide range of applications. It may be used to code a microprocessor or to create an operating system from the ground up. This book aims to provide a simple and easy-to-understand introduction to the C language.

This book aims to be an ultimate guide for keen and interested programmers to be, providing an informative outlook with an in-depth focus in a suitable flow with straightforward communication with organized chapters.

C programming for Beginners guides you through the fundamentals of programming and demonstrates how to put them into practice in C. As you go through the book, you'll be creating and running programs that use a variety of C-related concepts, such as program structure with functions (including data types) and conditional expressions. You'll learn how to utilize loops and iteration, as well as arrays, pointers, and strings, among other things. The topics covered will include code specification, testing and validation techniques, basic input/output, and how to construct entire programs in C as you advance through the course.

If you're a complete novice with just rudimentary knowledge of computer operation, this book will assist you in learning the essential ideas and techniques you'll need to know to become a good C programmer.

The whole spectrum of C language, as well as typical C idioms, will be available to you if you are an established programmer. You may quickly read over the explanations and concentrate mostly on the source code that has been made available.

All one needs to know about C programming is covered in this book, including the kinds of data and how they interact with the operators and statements that go with them. All are covered in this book without requiring you to put in long hours of studying computer science theory. This volume is a great place to start if you're new to C.

Chapter 1: C Fundamentals

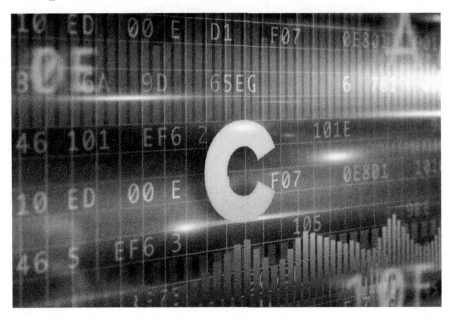

1.1: What is C?

C is a high-level programming dialect that is used for computer programming. This implies that you can use C to generate lists of instructions that a computer can follow and execute. Thousands of computer languages are presently in use, and C is only one of them. C has been around for many decades and has gained broad recognition since it provides programmers with the greatest amount of control and efficiency. C is a simple programming language to learn. This language is a little more mysterious in its approach than other languages, but once you get over that, it becomes rather simple.

C is an overall language of programming that is incredibly popular due to the fact that it is easy to learn and use while being easy and straightforward. C is a compiled language that is independent and is often released in the making of many OS, software apps, and numerous other abstract programs like the Oracle database and the Python interpreter, Git repository, and others.

It is claimed that the computer language 'C' was created by the gods. C is sometimes referred to be the "foundation language" of programming. If you are acquainted with the programming language 'C,' you will find it relatively easy to pick up on the concepts of the other computer languages that make use of the 'C' notion.

When working with the C language, it is crucial to have a solid understanding of computer retention systems since this is an important factor to consider.

C is what is referred to as a compiled programming language. This implies that after you have written your C program, you must pass it via a C compiler for it to be converted into an exe that can be launched by the computer. The C program is the true form, while the executable that is produced by the compiler is both the machine-readable and practical form of the program. This implies that to develop and execute a C program, you will need to have a relationship with a C compiler on your computer. UNIX machines are free to use, and the C compiler is accessible for download if you are using one (for example, if you are creating CGI programs in C on your host's UNIX machine or if you are a student on a lab's UNIX system). It is referred to as either "cc" or "gcc" and is accessible through the command-line interface. If you are a pupil, your school will almost certainly give you a compiler; find out what compiler your school is using and get familiar with it. If you are working from home on a Windows computer, you will need to either acquire a free C compiler or acquire a commercial compiler to complete your project. Microsoft's Visual environment (which generates both C and C++ applications) is a widely utilized compiler (that compiles C and C++ programs).

It uses many of the same principles as C++, including operators, control statements, data types, and others. The letter 'C' may be seen in a wide variety of uses. It is a straightforward expression that allows for quicker execution. In today's business, there are several opportunities for 'C' developers to further their careers.

The computer language 'C' is a compiled language in which a program is separated into several modules. Each component may be written independently, and when they are combined, they constitute a single 'C' program. Processes can be tested, maintained, and debugged more easily with this framework in place.

"C" features 32 keywords, a variety of data types, and a collection of sophisticated built-in functions that help programmers to be more productive.

Another advantage of 'C' programming; it is capable of self-extension. A 'C' program has a few functions that are all part of a library of functions. We have the ability to add our own features and functionality to the library. In your application, you can access and utilize these functions whenever you want. When handling such programming, this feature makes things a lot simpler.

There are a variety of compilers available on the market that may be used to execute programs written in this programming language.

Because it is a transportable language, applications developed in the 'C' programming language may be executed on a variety of different computers. This capability is required if we intend to utilize or execute code on a different machine from the one on which it was written.

A compiler is a complex tool that combines a program and turns it into what is called an object file that can be read by a computer's processor. Following the completion of the coding phase, the linker will join several object files into a single executable program that can be used to execute the program. The flow diagram hereunder displays the execution of a 'C' program in action.

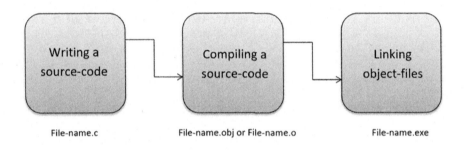

| Writing a source-code | Compiling a source-code | Linking object-files |
| File-name.c | File-name.obj or File-name.o | File-name.exe |

1.2: Uses of C

Learning C, which is considered to be one of the core programming languages, delivers a multitude of rewards to those who put in the effort to become proficient in it. The following are among the most significant benefits of learning C:

It will assist you in comprehending how a computer operates.

Understanding and visualizing the internal workings of computer networks (such as allocation and storage management), their design, and the overarching principles that drive programming will be made possible by studying C.

Because of its versatility as a computer language, C will enable you to create more complicated and complete programs.

It can be interacted with using the majority of programming languages.

JavaScript, Python, and Java, for example, are all high-level programming languages that can interact with C-based systems in a wide variety of ways. Consider Cython, a famous C-extension to Python that allows you to execute methods written in C and declare C types on variable and class properties, among other things. Additionally, due to its universal nature, C may be incredibly effective when attempting to express concepts and ideas in programming, which can be extremely beneficial.

You'll have the opportunity to contribute to open-source projects.

Despite the fact that many applications use a range of programming languages in addition to C, quite a number of those languages draw inspiration from C. In order to help millions of programmers across the globe, studying C will enable you to work on huge open-source projects, such as contributing to the Python source code, which will benefit from your knowledge of the language.

It will be less difficult to learn different programming languages in the future.

Being that C is the foundation of or intricately connected to so many other programming languages, your understanding of C will facilitate the experience of learning languages much easier. The syntax, operators, monitor measures, data types, and other features of these languages are often the same.

Testing and debugging are made easier by the structure.

This means that data objects and variables must be defined ahead of time in the C programming language, which is a highly typed language. As a result, the translator is able to impose appropriate use of these defined types and detect a number of problems throughout the compilation process.

Additional features include the idea of structures that are client types of data that may be used to organize data and code in an enabled firm. They may be developed separately and then integrated to make more complicated and bigger software... It is quite simple to analyze problems, delete them, and keep the software up to date as a result of this segmented structure, which increases the efficiency of testing.

It is a programming language with high efficiency.

C has just 32 keywords and also built-in procedures and data types, and it is an extraordinarily little language. C programs also include the functionality of functions that may be called by other programs and different interfaces to all of the functional requirements at any time in the program's execution.

The combination of all of these characteristics makes C both fast and straightforward to work with, which is particularly useful when designing complicated applications. Furthermore, C is a very efficient programming language, resulting in built binaries that run rapidly and with little overhead.

Also used in:

- Database systems and other applications are further examples of this term.

- Graphics software packages

- Personal computers with word processors

- Spreadsheets are used for a variety of purposes.

- Development of an operating system

- Computer programs that compile and assemble

- Drivers for networks

- Interpreters

1.3: Compilers and Installation

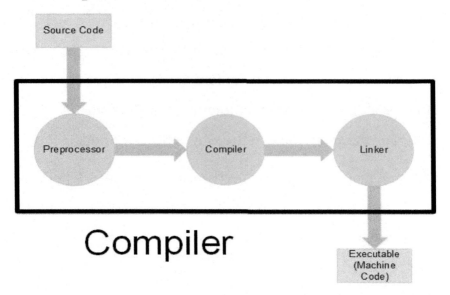

Compiler

Let's look at an example to better understand the notion of compilers. Consider the following scenario: you have travelled to a country where the dialects you speak are entirely different from one another, and you are now experiencing travel difficulties and want to converse in the same language as your companions. How? Did you need the services of a translator, correct? You choose to have somebody who understands your language interpret for you, allowing the other person to comprehend what you are trying to communicate to them. In a similar vein, we would write your C code in such a high-level form that it is easy to grasp for a human reader. What is the likelihood that the software will comprehend what we have requested it to do? It is at this point that the compiler enters the picture. A compiler is a program that converts and translates a high-level programming language into a machine-understandable programming language. The compiling process performs the fundamental translation mechanisms as well as error detection and correction. In addition to lexical and syntactic analysis, the front-end compiler provides semantic analysis. And the compilation is responsible for the programming and enhancement at the back end.

An integrated development environment (IDE) is an app or software that a programmer uses to accomplish programming. It provides programmers with all of the tools and resources they need to create a program or piece of software in general. It makes your coding job easier since it has built-in capabilities like code completion, debugging, compilation, and syntax highlighting, among other things. Would a programmer make use of an integrated development environment (IDE)? Its solution is straightforward. An integrated development environment (IDE) may raise the efficiency of a programmer since it has a variety of helpful tools and is simple to set up. A programmer's time may be suggestively increased if he or she does not use an IDE.

An integrated development environment (IDE) consists of three components: a compiler, a source code editor, and a debugger. What is a programming editor, and how does it work? The situation is one in which a programmer may develop a program (or code). The compiler is used to assemble the code, while the debug is used for debugging the program in order to identify and correct any issues that may have occurred during the compilation process. An integrated development environment (IDE) includes many useful extra features like object modelling, data modelling, unit testing, a source code library, and so on.

VS Code

In this book, you will be taught how to use VS Code for Implementing C programming.

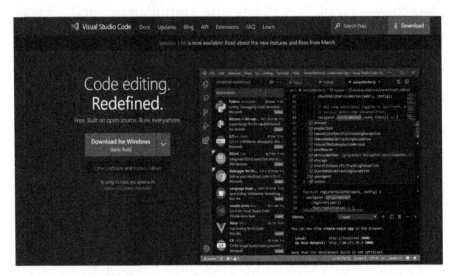

Visit the Visual Studio Code Website and download the file according to your system requirements.

Microsoft's VS Code is an efficient software tool that includes a strong source code editor and runs on the Windows operating system. It is a free computer code editor created by Microsoft for use with Windows, Mac OS, and Linux. It may be downloaded from the Microsoft website. Software editor with extensive language support for multiple programming languages such as C++, C+++, C (including Java), Python (including PHP and Go), and dynamic language extensions such as.NET and Unity (among others). Editing, syntax highlighting, building, snippets, code restructuring, and debugging are all simple tasks. Visual studio code allows us to customize the app's backdrop theme, keyboard shortcuts, and extra functionality. We can also install extensions and add new features.

Install the C/C++ Extension on your computer. It is a Microsoft-provided extension that allows for the support of Visual Studio code. The Visual Studio programming code benefits from the use of IntelliSence as well as debug and coding viewing capabilities.

Install the C/C++ compilers on your computer. Some of the most well-known compilers are as follows:

- GCC on Linux is a cross-platform compiler.

- On Windows, GCC is run using Mingw-w64.

- Compiler for the Microsoft C++ language on Windows

- Compiling Clang for use with XCode on MacOS

On this system, you must already have the VS Code environment for development. The following is how the Visual Studio Code user interface appears:

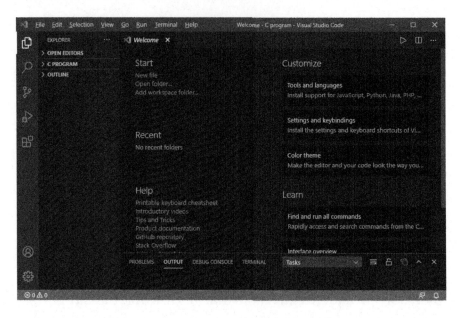

Download and install the C/C++ Extension

Clicking on the extension button will provide a sidebar that will allow us to download and install the C/C++ plugin in the Visual Studio Code environment. C Extension may be found on the sidebar by typing it in.

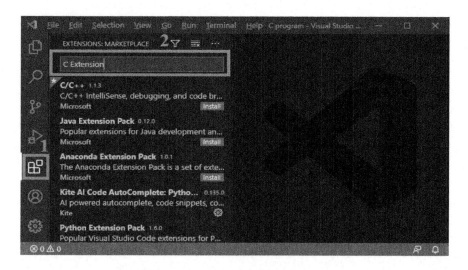

1. Click on the first one and install

2. The following should be visible

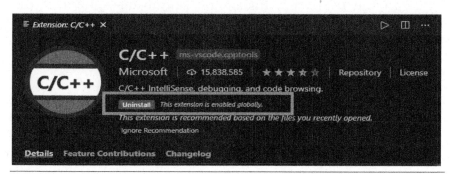

To use the Compiler Extension, you must download and install

Compiling and executing code can be done with MinGW, a developed GCC compiler software. It is a piece of software that only works with Windows.

1. First, go to the Mingw website at https://sourceforge.net and arrive at the next page.

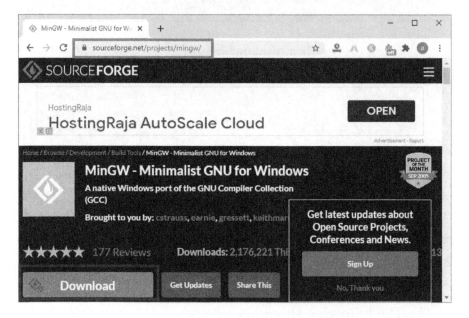

2. In the next step, install the plugin, as shown in the following picture, and the download of the MinGW GCC compiler will begin.

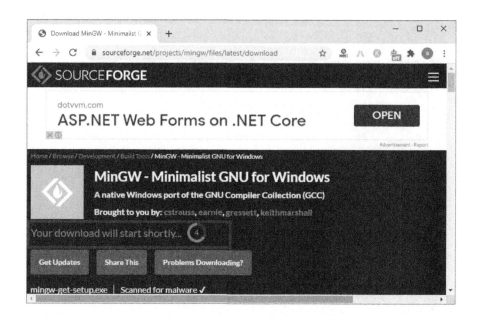

3. A successful download of the MinGW package has occurred.

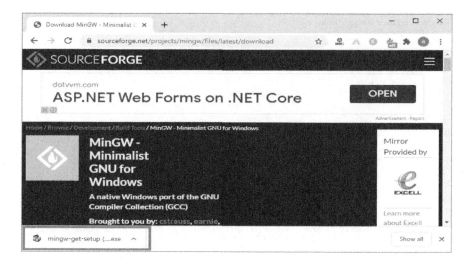

4. Double-clicking the MinGW setup will begin the compiler installation process.

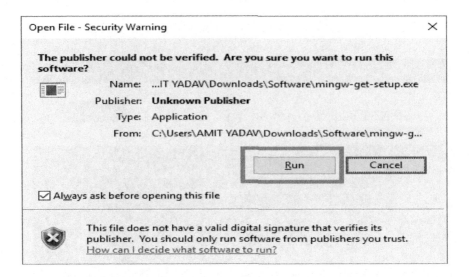

5. To begin with, the installation, click on the Launch button shown in the screenshot.

6. Press the Install button.

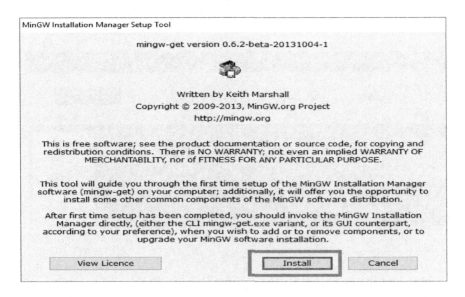

7. Change the setup's storage location if you choose. Then User has to click.

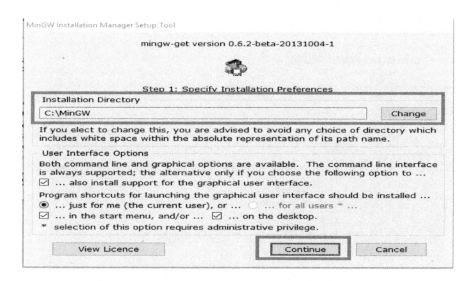

8. Step 2 of the MinGW Installation Manager appears after pressing the proceed button.

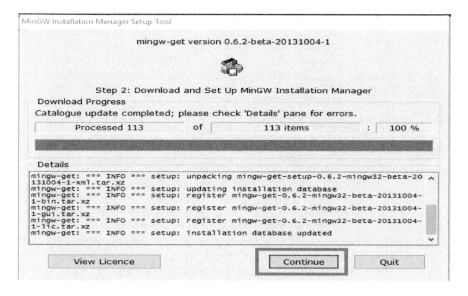

9. Clicking on Continue displays the picture below. In the MinGW Installation Manager, you have to select the Mingw32-base packages and Ming32-gcc-g++ package

to execute and build the C/ C++ program in the visual studio code editor.

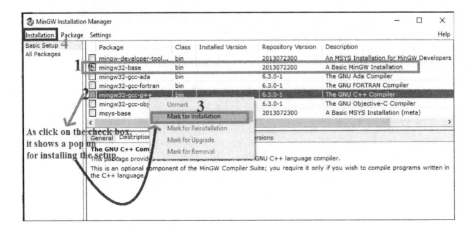

10. Select the Installation tab after checking the box

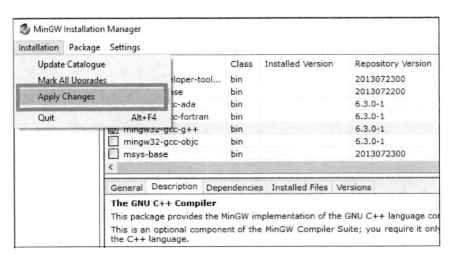

11. To configure the MinGW installation of the package, you tap on Apply Changes here.

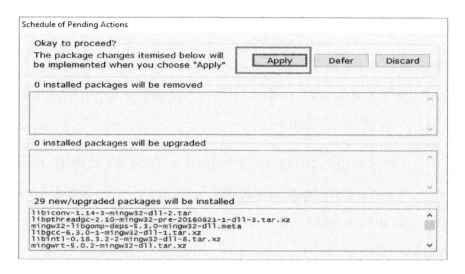

Schedule of Pending Actions

Okay to proceed?

The package changes itemised below will be implemented when you choose "Apply"

[Apply]   Defer   Discard

0 installed packages will be removed

0 installed packages will be upgraded

29 new/upgraded packages will be installed

```
libiconv-1.14-3-mingw32-dll-2.tar
libpthreadgc-2.10-mingw32-pre-20160821-1-dll-3.tar.xz
mingw32-libgomp-deps-5.3.0-mingw32-dll.meta
libgcc-6.3.0-1-mingw32-dll-1.tar.xz
libintl-0.18.3.2-2-mingw32-dll-8.tar.xz
mingwrt-5.0.2-mingw32-dll.tar.xz
```

12. After pressing the Apply button, the following picture appears.

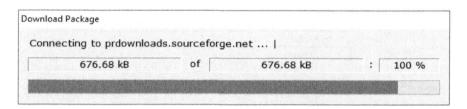

Download Package

Connecting to prdownloads.sourceforge.net ... |

| 676.68 kB | of | 676.68 kB | : | 100 % |

13. As soon as you have downloaded the packages, you will see the installation procedure as shown below.

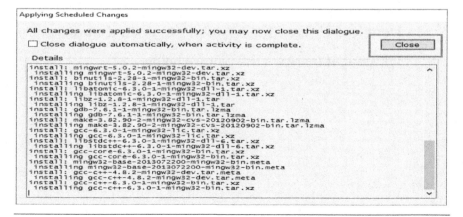

Applying Scheduled Changes

All changes were applied successfully; you may now close this dialogue.

☐ Close dialogue automatically, when activity is complete.

[Close]

Details

```
install: mingwrt-5.0.2-mingw32-dev.tar.xz
 installing mingwrt-5.0.2-mingw32-dev.tar.xz
install: binutils-2.28-1-mingw32-bin.tar.xz
 installing binutils-2.28-1-mingw32-bin.tar.xz
install: libatomic-6.3.0-1-mingw32-dll-1.tar.xz
 installing libatomic-6.3.0-1-mingw32-dll-1.tar.xz
install: libz-1.2.8-1-mingw32-dll-1.tar
 installing libz-1.2.8-1-mingw32-dll-1.tar
install: gdb-7.6.1-1-mingw32-bin.tar.lzma
 installing gdb-7.6.1-1-mingw32-bin.tar.lzma
install: make-3.82.90-2-mingw32-cvs-20120902-bin.tar.lzma
 installing make-3.82.90-2-mingw32-cvs-20120902-bin.tar.lzma
install: gcc-6.3.0-1-mingw32-llc.tar.xz
 installing gcc-6.3.0-1-mingw32-llc.tar.xz
install: libstdc++-6.3.0-1-mingw32-dll-6.tar.xz
 installing libstdc++-6.3.0-1-mingw32-dll-6.tar.xz
install: gcc-core-6.3.0-1-mingw32-bin.tar.xz
 installing gcc-core-6.3.0-1-mingw32-bin.tar.xz
install: mingw32-base-2013072200-mingw32-bin.meta
 installing mingw32-base-2013072200-mingw32-bin.meta
install: gcc-c++-4.8.2-mingw32-dev.tar.meta
 installing gcc-c++-4.8.2-mingw32-dev.tar.meta
install: gcc-c++-6.3.0-1-mingw32-bin.tar.xz
 installing gcc-c++-6.3.0-1-mingw32-bin.tar.xz
```

Set the MinGW Setup Environment Path.

The MinGW compiler has now been downloaded and installed, and the environment path has been modified to include the C/C++ compiler directory.

1. Go to the directory where the MinGW Setup was installed in Step 1. As can be seen in the screenshots below, we placed the setup on the C drive.

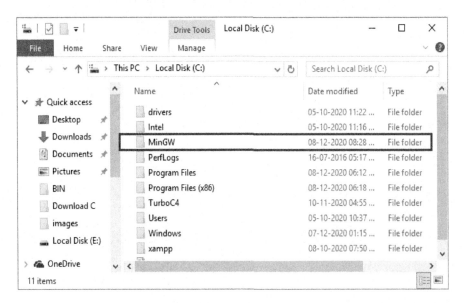

2. Double-click the MinGW folder to open it up in a new window. It displays the picture below.

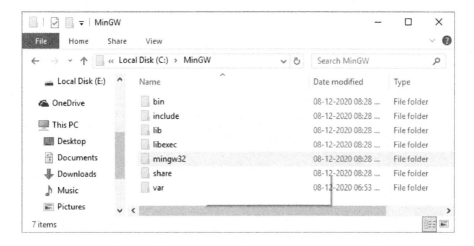

3. Following that, get on the bin folder and so copy the directory path, as seen in the following image.

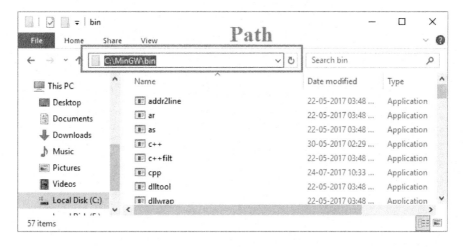

4. The path to the MinGW folder is as follows: C:\MinGW\bin

5. Go to This PC, then Right Click on This PC. Lastly, Select/Click on the Properties after copying the directory path. It displays the picture seen below.

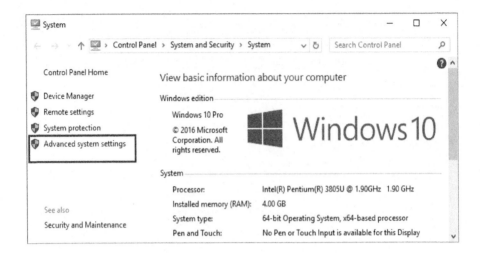

6. Click on Advanced system settings to bring up the System Properties window, as seen in the screenshot below.

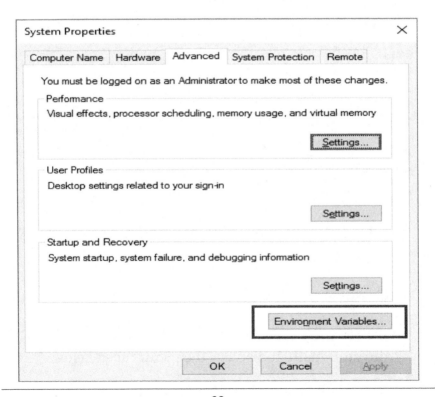

7. The directory path may be set by selecting Environment Variables from the context menu.

8. After selecting the System Variables Path, we must click on the Edit button, as seen in this figure.

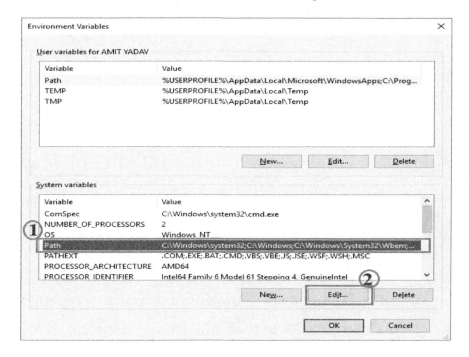

9. The Edit button opens a popup window where we may choose a new route.

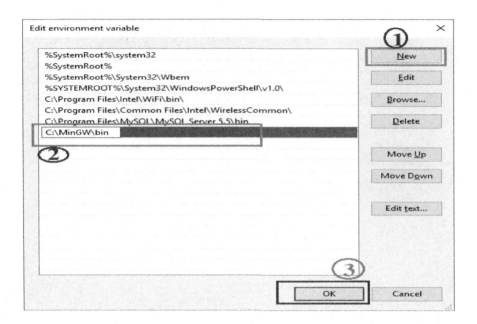

10. We begin by clicking on the New button and then entering the C:MinGWbin path; next, we press the OK button to finish.

11. In the Environment Variables and System Properties window, click OK to confirm your selections and go on.

12. To see whether the MinGW has been installed successfully, type gcc-version in the Command Prompt or cmd and hit Enter.

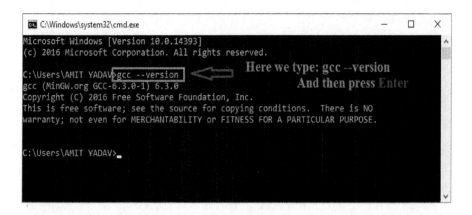

Use the Visual Studio Code Editor to get started coding.

1. To keep track of all the program codes, we established a C Programs folder in this location. In any directory, any name may be given to a folder.

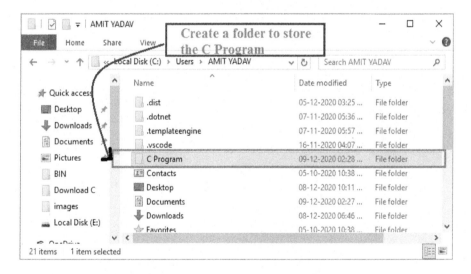

2. When you open VS Code, choose the Add Folder option.

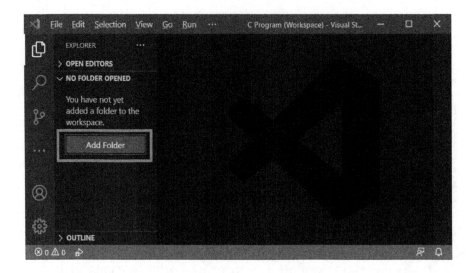

3. When we click on the Add Folder button, a pop-up
   window appears where we can pick the location where
   you save the application.

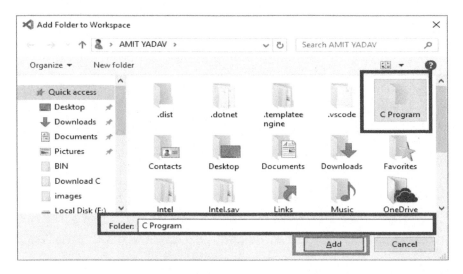

4. When you've chosen the folder, click the Add button.
   You can see the selected folder in the explorer section, as
   shown in the screenshots to the right.

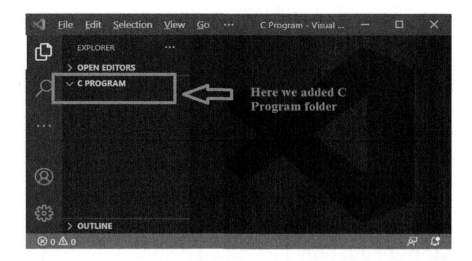

5. Click on the + button that appears when you hover over the C PROGRAM folder with the mouse and type in the filename hello.c like so.

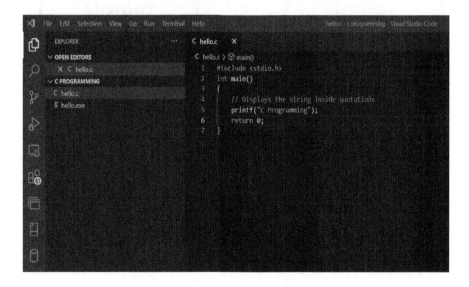

Chapter 2: First Program

2.1: Input/Output

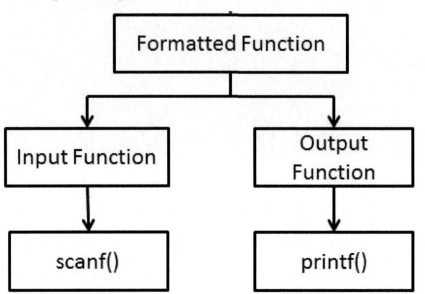

C Output:

The printf() function is amongst the most often used output functions in C programming. When this function is called, the formatted output is shown on the screen. As an example,

Example 1: C Output

#include <stdio.h>

int main()

{

// Displays the string inside the quotation marks

```c
printf("C Programming");

return 0;

}
```

Output:

```
C Programming
```

What is the procedure for implementing this program?

- Every legitimate C program must include a main() function. From the main() function begins the execution of the code.

- printf() is a standard library function that is used to produce formatted text for the screen. The function returns the string enclosed in quotation marks.

- You must include the <stdio.h> header file in our application to use printf() in our program.

- The return 0; expression included inside the main() method indicates the program's "Exit status." It is entirely optional.

Example 2: Integer Output

```c
#include <stdio.h>

int main()
```

```c
{

int cInteger = 8;

printf("Number = %d", cInteger);

return 0;

}
```

Output:

```
Number = 8
```

When printing int types, make use of the %d format specifier. The value for cInteger will be substituted for the %d contained inside the quotes in this case.

Example 3: float and double Output

```c
#include <stdio.h>

int main()

{

float num1 = 14.5;

double num2 = 10.4;

printf("num1 = %f\n", num1);

printf("num2 = %lf", num2);

return 0;
```

}

Output:

```
num1 = 14.500000
num2 = 10.400000
```

The %f format specifier prints the float value. Similarly, double numbers may be displayed by using %lf.

Example 4: Print Characters

```
#include <stdio.h>

int main()

{

char chr1 = 'b';

printf("character = %c", chr1);

return 0;

}
```

Output:

```
character = b
```

The %c format specifier is utilized to print char.

C Input:

scanf() is among the most widely used functions in C programming, which is used to take input from the user. Using the scanf() method, you may read formatted data from conventional input devices like keyboards.

Example 5: Integer Input/Output

```c
#include <stdio.h>

int main()
{
    int cInteger;

    printf("Please enter an integer: ");

    scanf_s("%d", &cInteger);

    printf("Number = %d", cInteger);

    return 0;
}
```

Output:

```
Please enter an integer: 8
Number = 8
```

Using the %d format specifier may accept int user input using the scanf() method shown above. When a user inputs an integer, the value is saved in the cInteger variable of the program. Additionally, the &cInteger is used inside scanf () because &cInteger obtains the address for cInteger, as well as the value given by the user, which is saved in that address.

Example 6: Float and Double Input/Output

```c
#include <stdio.h>

int main()
{
float number1;

double number2;

printf("Please enter a number: ");

scanf_s("%f", &number1);

printf("Please enter another number: ");

scanf_s("%lf", &number2);

printf("number1 = %f\n", number1);

printf("number2 = %lf", number2);

return 0;
}
```

Output:

```
Please enter a number: 9.89
Please enter another number: 17.1
number1 = 9.890000
number2 = 17.100000
```

For float and double, the %f and %lf format specifiers are utilized, respectively.

Example 7: C Character I/O

```
#include <stdio.h>

int main()

{

char chr1;

printf("Please enter a character: ");

scanf_s("%c", &chr1);

printf("You have entered %c.", chr1);

return 0;

}
```

Output:

```
Please enter a character: n
You have entered n.
```

The character is not saved when the user enters a character into the preceding application. Rather than that, an integer (ASCII value) is kept. And when the %c text format is used to represent that number, the input character is displayed. %d is used to show a character, and the ASCII value of the character is displayed.

Example 8: ASCII Value

```
#include <stdio.h>
```

```c
int main()

{

char chr1;

printf("Please enter a character: ");

scanf("%c", &chr1);

// %c is used to display a character

printf("You have entered %c.\n", chr1);

// %d is used to display the ASCII value

printf("ASCII value is %d.", chr1);

return 0;

}
```

Output:

```
Please enter a character: j
You have entered j.
ASCII value is 106.
```

I/O Multiple Values:

Here's how you accept numerous user inputs and display them.

Example:

```c
#include <stdio.h>

int main()
```

```c
{
int x;

    float y;

printf("Please first enter an integer and then a float: ");

// Taking multiple inputs

scanf_s("%d%f", &x, &y);

printf("You have entered %d and %f", x, y);

return 0;

}
```

Output:

```
Please first enter an integer and then a float: 6 7.9
You have entered 6 and 7.900000
```

2.2: Variables

A variable is a containment (storage space) for data in programming. Each variable must be given a distinct name to denote the storage region (identifier). Variable names are nothing more than a symbol for a memory location.

Type	Definition	Control Character	Limits
int	Integer		-2147483648 to 2147483647
short	Short Integer		-32768 to 32767
long	Long Integer	l or L	-2147483648 to 2147483647
float	Floating Decimal Number	f or F	1.17549e-038 to 3.40282e+038
double	Double Decimal Number		2.22507e-308 to 1.79769e+308
long double	Long Decimal Number		2.22507e-308 to 1.79769e+308
char	Character		-128 to 127
unsigned int	Unsigned Integer		0 to 4294967295
unsigned short	Unsigned Short Integer		0 to 65535
unsigned long	Unsigned Long Integer		0 to 4294967295
unsigned char	Unsigned Character		0 to 255
bool	True or False		True = 1 and False = 0

Example 1:

#include <stdio.h>

int main()

{

    int playerPoints = 95;

}

playerPoints is an int-type variable in this case. Here the variable is given the integer value 95.

A variable's value may be altered; that's why it is called a variable.

Example 2:

#include <stdio.h>

```c
int main()

{

    char chr = 'a';

    // some code

    chr = 'l';

}
```

Variable naming guidelines:

1. A variable name cannot include characters other than letters (including capital and lowercase), numerals, or underscore.

2. A variable's initial letter should be either an underscore or a letter.

3. No limitation on the length of a variable name (identifier). However, if the variable name exceeds 31 characters, you may have issues with certain compilers.

4. You should always attempt to give variables meaningful names. For instance, firstName is a more appropriate variable name than fn.

C is a statically typed programming language. This implies that it cannot be modified once a variable is defined.

Example 3:

```c
#include <stdio.h>

int main()

{

    int num = 5;     // integer variable

    num = 5.5;       // error

    double num;      // error

}
```

The type of the num variable is int in this case. This variable cannot be assigned the floating-point (decimal) value of 5.5. Additionally, you cannot change the variable's data type to double. By the way, in order to hold decimal values in C, one must designate their type as double or float.

Variable Types in C:

In c, there are several sorts of variables:

1. Local Variable

A variable defined inside a block or function is referred to as a local variable. It must be disclosed at the block's commencement.

Example 4:

```c
#include <stdio.h>

int main()
{
    void cfunction();
    {
        int x = 10;//local variable
    }
}
```

Before using the local variable, it must be initialized.

2. Global Variable

A global variable is well-defined outside of a function or block. Any function can modify the global variable's value. It is accessible via all functionalities. It must be disclosed at the block's commencement.

Example 5:

```c
#include <stdio.h>

int x = 20;//global variable

void cfunction1()
{
```

```c
    printf("%d\n", x);

}

void cfunction2()

{

    printf("%d\n", x);

}

int main() {


    cfunction1();

    cfunction2();

    return 0;

}
```

Output:

```
20
20
```

3. Static Variable

A variable defined using the static keyword is referred to as a static variable. It preserves its value throughout function calls.

Example 6:

#include <stdio.h>

```c
void cfunction() {

    int x = 10;//local variable

    static int y = 20;//static variable

    x = x + 10;

    y = y + 10;

    printf("\n%d,%d\n", x, y);
}
int main() {


    cfunction();

    cfunction();

    cfunction();

    return 0;

}
```

Output:

```
20,30
20,40
20,50
```

In the above example, local variables will always display the same value every time the function is called, but static variables will output the value that has been incremented with each function call.

4. Automatic Variable

By default, all variables defined inside a block in C are automatic variables. Using the auto keyword, you may specify an automatic variable explicitly.

Example 7:

```
#include <stdio.h>


int main()

{

    int x = 10;//local variable (also automatic)

    auto y = 20;//automatic variable

}
```

5. External Variable

You may share a variable across many C source files by utilizing an external variable. The extern keyword must be used to define an external variable

Example 8:

cfile.h

extern int x= 10;//external variable (also global)

program.c

#include "cfile.h"

#include <stdio.h>

void printVal()

{

   printf("Global variable: %d", global_variable);

}

2.3: Comments

Comments are indications that a programmer might include in their code to make it simpler to read and comprehend.

Example 1:

#include <stdio.h>

int main()

{

```c
// print Hello World to the screen

printf("Hello World");

return 0;

}
```

Output:

```
Hello World
```

// print Hello World on the screen is a C programming comment in this case. C compilers entirely disregard comments.

Comment Types:

1. Single-line C-Comments

A single-line comment in C begins with //. It starts and finishes off on the same line.

Example 2:

```c
#include <stdio.h>

int main()

{

// create an integer variable

int age = 25;
```

```c
// print the age variable

printf("Age: %d\n", age);

return 0;
}
```

Output:

```
Age: 25
```

// construct integer variable and // display the age variable is 2 single comments in the preceding example.

Additionally, you may utilize the single-line comment in conjunction with the code.

Example 3:

```c
#include <stdio.h>


int main()
{
    int age = 25; // create integer variable
}
```

The compiler executes the code before // and ignores the code after //.

2. Multi-line C-Comments

There is another sort of remark in C programming that enables us to comment on numerous lines simultaneously; these are called multi-line comments. You may utilize the /*....*/ sign to create multi-line comments.

Example 4:

/* This program takes age as input from the user

It stores it in the age variable

And prints the value using printf() */

#include <stdio.h>

int main()

{

    int age;

    printf("Enter the age: ");

    scanf_s("%d", &age);

```
printf("Age = %d", age);



return 0;

}
```

Output:

```
Enter the age: 23
Age = 23
```

The C compiler dismisses anything between /* and */ in this form of a remark.

Utilization of Comments in C:

1. Make Code More Understandable

By adding comments to our code, one can make it simpler to comprehend in the future. Otherwise, you'll spend lots of time debugging and attempting to grasp your code. Comments become much more critical while working in a team. It simplifies the process of other developers comprehending and using your code.

2. Making use of Comments to aid in Debugging

While debugging, there may be instances where you do not want to run a certain section of code. For instance, imagine you don't need height data in the program below. Thus, you can change the height-related code to comments rather than eliminate the height-related code.

Example 5:

```c
// Program to take age and height as input
#include <stdio.h>


int main()
{


    int age;
    // double height;


    printf("Enter the age: ");
    scanf_s("%d", &age);


    // printf("Enter the height: ");
    // scanf("%lf", &height);
```

```c
    printf("Age = %d", age);

    // printf("\nHeight = %.1lf", height);


    return 0;

}
```

Output:

```
Enter the age: 23
Age = 23
```

If you ever want more height, all you have to do is drop the forward slashes. Additionally, they will become assertions rather than comments.

2.4: Hello World

C "Hello, World!" Program:

You will be taught to create a C system to display the message "Hello, World!" on the screen in the illustration below.

Program to Output "Hello, World!":

```c
#include <stdio.h>

int main()

{
```

// printf() displays the string inside the quotation

printf("Hello, World!\n");

return 0;

}

Output:

```
Hello, World!
```

How does the "Hello, World!" program function?

- The preprocessor instruction #include instructing the compiler to incorporate the contents of the stdio.h (standard input & output) file in the program's source code.

- This file, which provides methods like scanf() and printf(), allows you to take in data and show it on the screen.

- Suppose you utilize the printf() routine without including the stdio.h header file, the application will not compile correctly.

- The main() function is where the C program's execution begins.

- It is possible to deliver formatted output to the desktop using the printf() function, which is a library function. This program's printf() function shows the words "Hello, World!" on the screen.

- The return 0; statement indicates that the program has reached its "Exit status." In layman's terms, this sentence signifies the conclusion of the program.

Chapter 3: Data Types

Data Type	Format	Meaning
int	%d	Represents a decimal integer value.
	%u	Represents an unsigned integer value.
	%o	Represents an unsigned octal value.
	%x	Represents an unsigned hexadecimal value.
float	%f	Represents a floating point value.
	%e	Represents a floating point value in decimal or exponential form.
char	%c	Represents a single character value.
	%s	Represents a string of value of characters.

3.1: Initialization

Numerous methods for initializing a variable in C:

Variables are random names assigned to a memory region in the computer's memory. These memory locations are the addresses of memory regions in the computer. Let's say you wish to keep track of our grades in your heads. Now, these marks will be recorded at a specific location in the computer's memory. Now, whenever these markings are changed, they will be saved at a different storage location than they were before. In order to make the retrieval of these memory locations more convenient, variables are used. Variables are the names that have been assigned to various memory regions. This variable refers to a memory region with a particular value relevant to us. In order to assign a value to these variables, they must first be defined. Initialization of variables refers to assigning a value to variables that have not yet been assigned.

There are two forms of variable initialization:

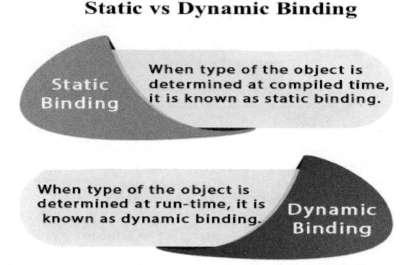

- Static Initialization

The variable is given a value beforehand in this case. As a result, this variable serves as a constant.

- Dynamic Initialization:

The variable is given a value at runtime in this case. Every time the program is executed, the value of such a variable may be changed.

The following are various C methods for initializing a variable:

Method 1 (Declaring and then initializing the variable):

Example 1:

```
#include <stdio.h>

int main()

{

    int a;

    a = 5;

}
```

Method 2 (Concurrently declaring and initializing the variable):

Example 2:

```
#include <stdio.h>

int main()

{

    int a = 5;

}
```

Method 3 (Multiple variables are declared concurrently and then initialized individually):

Example 3:

```c
#include <stdio.h>

int main()
{
    int a, b;
    a = 5;
    b = 10;
}
```

Method 4 (Declaring and initializing many variables concurrently):

Example 4:

```c
#include <stdio.h>

int main()
{
    int a, b;
    a = b = 10;
}
```

Example 5:

```c
#include <stdio.h>
```

```c
int main()

{

    int a, b = 10, c = 20;

}
```

Method 6 (Dynamic Initialization: Value is allocated to a variable at runtime.):

Example 6:

```c
#include <stdio.h>

int main()

{

    int a;

    printf("Enter the value of a: ");

    scanf_s("%d", &a);

    printf("The entered value of a is: %d\n", a);

}
```

Output:

```
Enter the value of a: 7
The enetered value of a is: 7
```

3.2: Character

The purpose here is to teach you about the C character type and how to define, utilize, and display character variables in C. The char type is used by C to hold characters and letters. Nevertheless, the char type is an integer type since C holds integer numbers rather than the characters below. The computer must use numerical code to indicate characters to translate each integer to a corresponding character. ASCII, which refers to American Standard Code for Information Interchange, is the most often used numerical code.

The ASCII code is shown in the following table:

*	0	1	2	3	4	5	6	7	8	9	A	B	C	D	E	F
0	NUL	SOH	STX	ETX	EOT	ENQ	ACK	BEL	BS	TAB	LF	VT	FF	CR	SO	SI
1	DLE	DC1	DC2	DC3	DC4	NAK	SYN	ETB	CAN	EM	SUB	ESC	FS	GS	RS	US
2		!	"	‡	$	%	&	'	(	)	*	+	,	-	.	/
3	0	1	2	3	4	5	6	7	8	9	:	;	<	=	>	?
4	@	A	B	C	D	E	F	G	H	I	J	K	L	M	N	O
5	P	Q	R	S	T	U	V	W	X	Y	Z	[	\	]	^	_
6	`	a	b	c	d	e	f	g	h	i	j	k	l	m	n	o
7	p	q	r	s	t	u	v	w	x	y	z	{			}	~	

For instance, the integer 65 symbolizes the upper case letter A.

The char type in C has a 1-byte memory unit, which is more than adequate to store the ASCII codes. Apart from ASCII codes, different numerical codes, like extended ASCII codes, are available. Regrettably, many character sets include more than 127 or even 255 characters. As a result, Unicode was designed to represent the numerous accessible character sets. At the moment, Unicode has about 40,000 characters.

Using C char type:

To define a variable of a type character, precede the variable name with the char keyword. Three char variables are declared in the following example.

Example 1:

```
#include <stdio.h>

int main()

{

    char ch;

    char key, flag;

}
```

You can use a character literal to initialize a character variable in this example. A single character literal is contained in a single quotation mark (').

The following example defines and initializes a key character variable using the character literal 'A':

Example 2:

```
#include <stdio.h>

int main()

{

    char key = 'A';

}
```

Since the char type is an integer, you may initialize or assign an integer to a char variable. However, it is not encouraged because the code might not be portable.

Example 3:

```
#include <stdio.h>

int main()

{

    ch = 66;

}
```

Displaying C character type:

You use the printf() method with the placeholder %c to print characters in C. If you are using %d, an integer will be returned rather than a character. The example below shows how to display characters in C.

Example 4:

```
#include <stdio.h>

int main()

{

    char ch = 'A';

    printf("ch = %c\n", ch);

    printf("ch = %d, hence an integer\n", ch);

    return 0;

}
```

Output:

```
ch = A
ch = 65, hence an integer
```

3.3: Integer

Int:

Integers are whole integers that may include zero, positive, or negative values but do not contain decimal values. For instance, 0, -5, and ten. You may declare an integer variable using int.

Example 1:

```
#include <stdio.h>
```

```
int main()

{

    int id;

}
```

Id is an integer-type variable in this case.

Multiple variables may be declared concurrently in C programming.

Example 2:

```
#include <stdio.h>

int main()

{

    int id, age;

}
```

Integers are typically 4 bytes in length (32 bits). Additionally, it may exist in 232 unique states between -2147483648 and 2147483647.

Integer Types:

Integer numbers are all-inclusive integers that include zero, negative, and positive values, such as 0, -1, 1, 2,... 2020. There is no decimal point in integer numbers. 3.14, for instance, is not an integer since it includes a decimal point. The integer type is represented in C via the int keyword. The following defines an integer-type variable:

Example 3:

```
#include <stdio.h>

int main()

{

    int age = 1;

}
```

Internally, C employs a fixed amount of bits (a sequence of 1 and 0) to hold integers. Additionally, the amount of bits varies from machine to computer. For instance, most UNIX workstations encode integers with 32 bits (4 bytes). Thus, the int numbers range from -232 (-2,147,483,648) to 231-1. (2,147,483,647). However, some outdated computers represent integers with 16 bits. As a result, the integers have a range of -32,768 to 32,767.

The limits. h file provides two values for the integers' maximum and minimum values. On your PC, the following software shows the integer range:

Example 4:

```c
#include <stdio.h>

#include <limits.h>

int main()

{

    printf("(%d, %d)\n", INT_MIN, INT_MAX);


    return 0;

}
```

Output:

```
(-2147483648, 2147483647)
```

Short / Long qualifiers:

C has two qualifiers, short and long, which modify the size of integers. Short is often 16 bits in length, whereas long is at most 32 bits. The principle is that short cannot exceed int, and int cannot exceed long. This, however, is contingent upon the compilers adhering to the norm.

Signed / unsigned integers:

Signed and unsigned are two integer qualifiers provided by C that may be applied to any integer. Unsigned integers are always zero and positive.

Example 5:

```
#include <stdio.h>

int main()

{

    unsigned int quanity = 20;


    signed int profit = 0;

}
```

Integer types and their accompanying synonyms are shown in the following table:

Integer Types	Synonyms
int	signed, signed int
short	short int, signed short, signed short int
long	long int, signed long, signed long int
long	long int, signed long, signed long int

The C programming language provides a comparable unsigned integer data type with the same memory footprint as each signed integer. Here is a table that shows the different unsigned integer types available:

Signed Integer Types	unsigned Integer Types
int	unsigned int
short	unsigned short
long	unsigned long
long	unsigned long

Ranges of integers:

C specifies the precise minimum storage size required by each integer type; for example, the short type requires at least 2 bytes of storage, and the long type requires at least 4 bytes of storage. The table below lists the most often encountered integer type sizes in C:

Type	Storage size	Minimum value	Maximum value
char	1 byte	-128	127
unsigned char	1 byte	0	255

Type	Storage size	Minimum value	Maximum value
signed char	1 byte	-128	127
int	2 bytes or 4 bytes	-32,768 or -2,147,483,648	-32,767 or 2,147,483,647
unsigned int	2 bytes or 4 bytes	0	65,535 or 2,147,483,647
short	2 bytes	-32,768	32,767
unsigned short	2 bytes	0	65,535
long	4 bytes	-2,147,483,648	2,147,483,647
unsigned long	4 bytes	0	4,294,967,295
long long(C99)	8 bytes	-9,223,372,036,854,775,808	9,223,372,036,854,775,807
unsigned long	8 bytes	0	18,446,744,073,709,551,615

Getting the sizes of integer types:

To find out the size of an integer data type, you may use the sizeof() operator, which returns the size of a class in bytes, as seen in the following example. Examples of such programs include the following program, which utilizes the sizeof() method to determine the sizes of different integer types:

```c
#include <stdio.h>

int main()
{

    printf("sizeof(short) = %d bytes\n", sizeof(short));

    printf("sizeof(int) = %d bytes\n", sizeof(int));

    printf("sizeof(signed int) = %d bytes\n", sizeof(signed int));

    printf("sizeof(long) = %d bytes\n", sizeof(long));

    printf("sizeof(long long) = %d bytes\n", sizeof(long long));

    return 0;

}
```

Output:

```
sizeof(short) = 2 bytes
sizeof(int) = 4 bytes
sizeof(signed int) = 4 bytes
sizeof(long) = 4 bytes
sizeof(long long) = 8 bytes
```

3.4: Floating-Point Types: Float double/Long double

Float and Double:

Real numbers are stored in the float and double types of variables.

Example 1:

#include <stdio.h>

int main()

{

    float salary;

    double price;

}

Floating-point numbers may also be expressed in C using exponential notation.

Example 2:

#include <stdio.h>

int main()

```
{

    float normalizationFactor = 22.442e2;

}
```

What is the difference between the terms float and double?

Float (single precision float type data) occupies four bytes. And double (double precision float type data) has an 8-byte capacity.

Data types for floating-point numbers:

Basic Floating point numbers - float:

Float requires a minimum of 32 bits to store but provides six decimal places between 1.2E-38 and 3.4E+38.

Doubles - double:

Doubles the memory capacity of float (so at least 64 bits). In exchange, double may supply a range of 15 decimal places between 2.3E-308 and 1.7E+308.

Increasing the range of possible doubles - long double:

A long double requires at least 80 bits. As a consequence, 19 decimal points between 3.4E-4932 and 1.1E+4932 are available.

The following example defines floating-point number variables using the float and double keywords:

Example 3:

```c
#include <stdio.h>

int main()

{

    float x = 0.1,

        y = 0.1,

        z = 0.1;


    float total = x + y + z;


    printf("The sum is %.20f\n", total);


    return 0;

}
```

Output:

```
The sum is 0.30000001192092895508
```

How does it work?

- To begin, define the three floating-point variables x, y, and z.

- Second, multiply three integers by themselves and show the result.

The total of 0.1, 0.1, and 0.1 equals 0.30000001192092896000, not 0.3. This is because floating-point numbers have a high degree of accuracy.

What is precision?

Consider the fraction 5/3. This value may be expressed in decimal form as 1.666666666... with an endless number of zeros. Due to the fact that computers use a limited amount of bits, they cannot store an endless number. Rather than that, computers precisely store these numbers. Precision is indicated in terms of significant digits. Accuracy is defined as the maximum number of digits a number may represent without sacrificing data.

For instance, the float type, which has four bytes = four x eight bits = 32 bits, is used for single-precision values. This implies that a float has one sign bit, eight exponent bits, and twenty-three significand bits. The double type represents a number with double precision, including one sign bit, 11 exponent bits, and 52 significant bits. (8 bytes x 8 bits = 64 bits, which is equal to 1 bit plus 52 bits plus 11 bits).

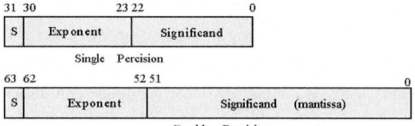

Single Precision

Double Precision

Short and Long qualifiers:

As with integers, you can specify the size of a floating-point class using the long and short qualifiers. The following table summarizes the many floating-point types available in C.

Type	Size	Ranges	Smallest Value	Positive	Precision
float	4 bytes	±3.4E+38	1.2E-38		6 digits
double	8 bytes	±1.7E+308	2.3E-308		15 digits
long double	10 bytes	±1.1E+4932	3.4E-4932		19 digits

It is critical to remember that this is merely the bare minimum storage size requirement specified by C.

Float ranges and precision:

The float.h header file may be used to determine the floating-point number's value ranges. This header file provides macros

Like FLT MIN, FLT MAX, and FLT DIG, which are used to hold the float type's float value precision and ranges. Additionally, float.h includes macros with the prefixes DBL_ & LDBL_ for double and long double. The following application displays your system's floating-point storage amount and accuracy.

Example 4:

```
#include <stdio.h>

#include <stdlib.h>

#include <limits.h>

#include <float.h>

int main(int argc, char** argv)

{
    printf("Storage size for float : %d \n", sizeof(float));

    printf("FLT_MAX   :  %g\n", (float)FLT_MAX);

    printf("FLT_MIN   :  %g\n", (float)FLT_MIN);

    printf("-FLT_MAX   :  %g\n", (float)-FLT_MAX);

    printf("-FLT_MIN   :  %g\n", (float)-FLT_MIN);

    printf("DBL_MAX   :  %g\n", (double)DBL_MAX);

    printf("DBL_MIN   :  %g\n", (double)DBL_MIN);

    printf("-DBL_MAX   :  %g\n", (double)-DBL_MAX);
```

```c
    printf("Precision value: %d\n", FLT_DIG);

    return 0;

}
```

Output:

```
Storage size for float : 4
FLT_MAX      :    3.40282e+38
FLT_MIN      :    1.17549e-38
-FLT_MAX     :    -3.40282e+38
-FLT_MIN     :    -1.17549e-38
DBL_MAX      :    1.79769e+308
DBL_MIN      :    2.22507e-308
-DBL_MAX     :    -1.79769e+308
Precision value: 6
```

3.5: Strings

A string is a sequence of literals terminated by the null character \0 in C programming.

Example 1:

```c
#include <stdio.h>

int main()

{

    char c[] = "c string";

}
```

When the compiler comes across a series of characters wrapped in double quotation marks, this defaults to appending the null character 0 at the end.

c		s	t	r	i	n	g	\0

What is the key approach to defining a string?

The following example illustrates how to define strings:

Example 2:

#include <stdio.h>

int main()

{

    char s[5];

}

s[0]	s[1]	s[2]	s[3]	s[4]

Here, a five-character string has been defined.

How should strings be initialized?

Strings may be initialized in a variety of ways.

Example 3:

```
#include <stdio.h>

int main()

{

    char c1[] = "abcd";


    char c2[50] = "abcd";


    char c3[] = { 'a', 'b', 'c', 'd', '\0' };


    char c4[5] = { 'a', 'b', 'c', 'd', '\0' };

}
```

c[0]	c[1]	c[2]	c[3]	c[4]
a	b	c	d	\0

Example 4:

```
#include <stdio.h>
```

```
int main()

{

   char c[5] = "abcde";

}
```

Here, one is attempting to assign six characters (the final character is '\0') to a five-character char array. This is unacceptable, and you must never do it.

Assigning Strings with Values:

In C, strings and arrays are second-class citizens; they do not support the project operator once defined.

Example 5:

```
#include <stdio.h>

int main()

{

   char c[100];

   c = "C programming"; // Error! an array type is not
assignable.

}
```

Read String from the user:

The scanf() method may be used to read a string from the user. The scanf() method scans the character sequence until it reaches whitespace (newline, space, tab, etc.).

Example 1: scanf() to read a string

```
#include <stdio.h>

int main()

{

    char name[40];

    printf("Please enter your name: ");

    scanf_s("%s", name);

    printf("Your name is %s.", name);

    return 0;

}
```

Output:

```
Please enter your name: John Fritz
Your name: John.
```

Although John Fritz was put into the preceding application, the name string included simply "John." That is because there was a

gap after John. Additionally, note that the code name is utilized rather than &name with scanf ().

scanf_s("%s", name);

It's because the name is a char array, and array names in C degrade to pointers. Thus, the label in scanf() already refers to the location of the string's first element, which eliminates the requirement for &.

Traversing String:

Traversing a string is a critical component of every programming language. You might need to manage an exceptionally long text, which may be accomplished using text traversal. Traversing a string differs somewhat from reading an integer array. To traverse a numeric array, you must know its length; however, in the case of a string, you can utilize the null character to identify the end of the string and finish the loop.

As a result, there are two distinct methods for traversing a string:

1. Utilizing the length of a string

Consider the following example for counting the vowels in a phrase.

Example 2:

```c
#include<stdio.h>
void main()
{
    char s[13] = "cprogramming";
    int i = 0;
    int count = 0;
    while (i < 13)
    {
        if (s[i] == 'a' || s[i] == 'e' || s[i] == 'i' || s[i] == 'u' || s[i] == 'o')
        {
            count++;
        }
        i++;
    }
```

```
    printf("The number of vowels is: %d\n", count);

}
```

Output:

```
The number of vowels is: 3
```

2. Utilizing the null character

Consider the same case of counting vowels with the null letter.

Example 3:

```
#include<stdio.h>
void main()
{
    char s[13] = "cprogramming";
    int i = 0;
    int count = 0;
    while (s[i] != NULL)
    {
        if (s[i] == 'a' || s[i] == 'e' || s[i] == 'i' || s[i] == 'u' || s[i] == 'o')
        {
```

```c
        count++;

    }

    i++;

}

    printf("The number of vowels is: %d\n", count);

}
```

Output:

```
The number of vowels is: 3
```

How to read a string?

The fgets() method may be used to read any line of text. Additionally, you may show the string using puts().

Example 4: fgets() and puts()

```c
#include <stdio.h>

int main()

{

    char name[30];

    printf("Enter name: ");

    fgets(name, sizeof(name), stdin);  // read string
```

```
printf("Name: ");

puts(name);   // display string

return 0;

}
```

Output:

The fgets() method has been used to retrieve a phrase from the user in this example.

fgets(name, sizeof(name), stdlin); // read string

The result of sizeof(name) is 30. As a result, you may accept up to 30 characters as input, which is the length of the name string.puts(name) is used; to output the text.

Additionally, the gets() method may be used to accept user input. It is, however, omitted from the C standard. This is because gets() accepts character strings of any length. A buffer overflow may occur as a result.

Passing Strings to Functions:

Strings, like arrays, may be supplied to a function.

Example 5: Passing string to a Function

```c
#include <stdio.h>

void displayString(char str[]);


int main()
{
    char str[50];

    printf("Enter string: ");

    fgets(str, sizeof(str), stdin);

    displayString(str);    // Passing string to a function.

    return 0;
}

void displayString(char str[])
{
    printf("String Output: ");

    puts(str);
}
```

Output:

```
Enter string: My name is Ali
String Output: My name is Ali
```

C provides a comprehensive set of functions for manipulating null-terminated strings:

Sr.No.	Function & Purpose
1	strcpy(s1, s2); String s2 is copied into string s1.
2	strcat(s1, s2); String s2 is appended to the end of string s1.
3	strlen(s1); The length of the string s1 is returned.
4	strcmp(s1, s2); Outputs 0 if s1 and s2 are equal; less than 0 if s1 is lesser than s2; greater than 0 if s1 is greater than s2.
5	strchr(s1, ch); This function returns a reference to the first instance of the character ch in the string s1.

6	strstr(s1, s2);
	This function returns a reference to the first instance of the string s2 in the string s1.

The example below makes use of some of the functions stated previously:

Example 6:

```
#include <stdio.h>

#include <string.h>


int main() {

    char str1[12] = "Hello";

    char str2[12] = "World";

    char str3[12];

    int  len;


    /* copy str1 into str3 */

    strcpy_s(str3, str1);

    printf("strcpy( str3, str1) :  %s\n", str3);
```

/* concatenates str1 and str2 */

strcat_s(str1, str2);

printf("strcat(str1, str2):   %s\n", str1);

/* total lenghth of str1 after concatenation */

len = strlen(str1);

printf("strlen(str1) :   %d\n", len);

    return 0;

}

Compiling and running the code above yields the following outcome:

Output:

```
strcpy( str3, str1) :   Hello
strcat( str1, str2):    HelloWorld
strlen(str1) :   10
```

Strings and Pointers:

String identifiers are "decayed" into pointers in the same way as array names are. As a result, manipulating the string's constituents is possible via the usage of pointers.

Example 7: Strings and Pointers

```c
#include <stdio.h>

int main(void)
{
    char name[] = "Harry Potter";

    printf("%c", *name);        // Output: H
    printf("%c", *(name + 1));  // Output: a
    printf("%c", *(name + 7));  // Output: o

    char* namePtr;

    namePtr = name;
    printf("%c", *namePtr);        // Output: H
    printf("%c", *(namePtr + 1));  // Output: a
    printf("%c\n", *(namePtr + 7)); // Output: o
}
```

Output:

3.6: Arrays

A form of data structure that may be used to hold a fixed-size sequential set of identical items is called an array. Although an array is employed to hold data, it is often more practical to conceive it as a group of variables of the same kind. Rather than defining variables like number0,.., and number98, declare a single array variable like a number and use number[0], numbers[1], and numbers[98] to indicate individual variables. An index is used to locate a particular element inside an array. All arrays are made up of adjacent memory regions. The first element is represented by the lowest address, while the final element is represented by the highest address.

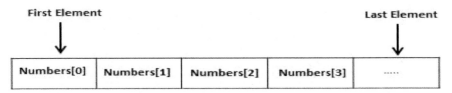

A variable that could hold numerous values is called an array. For instance, if you wish to hold 100 integers, you may do so by creating an array.

Example 1:

#include <stdio.h>

```
int main()

{

    int data[100];

}
```

What is the appropriate way to define an array?

```
dataType arrayName[arraySize];
```

Example 2:

```
#include <stdio.h>


int main()

{

    float mark[5];

}
```

Here, a floating-point array mark is defined. And it measures five inches in length. That is, it can store up to five floating-point numbers. It's critical to remember that its size and type cannot be modified once an array is defined.

Access Array Elements:

Indexes are used to access items in an array. Assume you've defined an array mark in the manner described above. The 1st element is denoted by mark[0], the second by mark[1], etc.

mark[0]	mark[1]	mark[2]	mark[3]	mark[4]

Few keynotes:

- Arrays begin with zero, not one. Mark[0] is the initial element in this example.

- If an array is of the length of n, the n-1 position is used to reach the last member. Mark[4] is a good illustration of this.

- Assume mark[0] has a beginning address of 2120d. The address[1] of the mark will then be 2124d. Similarly, mark[2address] will be 2128d, and so on.

This is because a float is 4 bytes in size.

What is the correct way to initialize an array?

Arrays may be initialized as part of the declaration process.

Example 3:

#include <stdio.h>

```
int main()

{

    int mark[5] = { 18, 11, 9, 16, 8 };

}
```

Another way to set up an array is illustrated in the example below.

Example 4:

```
#include <stdio.h>


int main()

{

    int mark[] = { 18, 11, 9, 16, 8 };

}
```

The dimensions have not been given in this case. On the other hand, the compiler knows its capacity is 5 since you're putting 5 items into it.

mark[0]	mark[1]	mark[2]	mark[3]	mark[4]
18	11	9	16	8

Here,

mark[0] is equal to 18

mark[1] is equal to 11

mark[2] is equal to 9

mark[3] is equal to 16

mark[4] is equal to 8

Modify Value of Array elements:

Example 5:

```c
#include <stdio.h>

int main()
{
    int mark[5] = { 18, 11, 9, 16, 8 };

    // set the third element's value to -1
    mark[2] = -1;

    // Set the fifth element's value to 0
    mark[4] = 0;
```

```
}
```

Input & Output Array Elements:

This example shows how to accept input from a user and save it in an array element.

Example 6:

```
// collect data and save it in the fourth element
scanf_s("%d", &mark[3]);
```

```
// collect and store the data in the ith array element
scanf_s("%d", &mark[i - 1]);
```

Here's how to print a single element from an array.

Example:

```
// print the first element of the array
printf("%d", mark[0]);
```

```
// print the third element of the array
printf("%d", mark[2]);
```

```c
// print ith element of the array

printf("%d", mark[i - 1]);
```

Example 7: Array Input/Output

```c
// A program that accepts 5 user-supplied values and stores
them in an array

// Print the array's elements

#include <stdio.h>


int main() {
    int values[5];


    printf("Enter 5 integers: ");


    // accumulating and saving data in an array
    for (int i = 0; i < 5; ++i) {
        scanf_s("%d", &values[i]);
    }


    printf("Displaying integers: ");
```

// printing elements of an array

for (int i = 0; i < 5; ++i) {

printf("%d\n", values[i]);

}

return 0;

}

Output:

```
Enter 5 integers: 1
2
3
4
5
Displaying integers: 1
2
3
4
5
```

Here a for loop has been utilized to collect five user inputs and save them in an array. These items are then shown on the screen using another loop.

Example 8: Calculate the Average

//program to determine the average of n integers using arrays

#include <stdio.h>

int main() {

```c
int marks[10], i, n, sum = 0, average;
printf("Enter number of elements: ");
scanf_s("%d", &n);

for (i = 0; i < n; ++i) {
    printf("Enter number%d: ", i + 1);
    scanf_s("%d", &marks[i]);

    // adding user-supplied numbers to the sum variable
    sum += marks[i];
}

average = sum / n;
printf("Average = %d", average);

return 0;
}
```

Output:

```
Enter number of elements: 6
Enter number1: 23
Enter number2: 45
Enter number3: 12
Enter number4: 15
Enter number5: 98
Enter number6: 66
Average = 43
```

The mean of n numbers provided by the user has been calculated here.

Access items that are not included inside its bounds!

Assume you've defined a ten-element array.

Let's say:

#include<stdio.h>

int main()

{

   int testArray[10];

}

From testArray[0] through testArray[9], you may access the array elements.

Now consider the case if you attempt to access testArray[12]. The item is not accessible at the moment. This might result in unpredictable output (undefined behaviour). Occasionally, you may get an error, but other times, your software may execute perfectly. As a result, you must never access an array's items outside of its bounds.

Arrays are critical to C and should get much more attention. A C programmer should understand the following critical array concepts:

Sr.No.	Concept & Description
1	Multi-dimensional arrays C allows for the creation of multidimensional arrays. The two-dimensional array is the simplest kind of multidimensional array.
2	Passing arrays to functions You may send a pointer to an array to the method by supplying the array's name without a reference.
3	Return array from a function

	C provides the ability for a procedure to output an array.
4	Pointer to an array You may produce a pointer to the array's first entry without any index by giving the array name alone.

Chapter 4: Conditional Statements

4.1: About Conditional Statements

Human humans created computer systems in order to make their lives more convenient for themselves. Computers make our lives simpler in a variety of ways that are too numerous to name. In order to do sophisticated ANOVA calculations, for example, computers are utilized, and computers are also used to operate software applications.

Because computers are incapable of reasoning according to themselves, and because humans want to entrust computers with the task of executing complicated and even basic tasks, software must be developed to operate on the computer network and provide specific instructions for it to follow. To be able to distinguish and understand the action that it is responsible for doing for its owner during any given moment. These objectives are achieved via the usage of programming languages.

Conditional statements, conditionals, or expressions are programming language elements that instruct the computer to do particular actions if certain circumstances are satisfied. They are also known as conditional logic.

Conditional statements are essential in the fields of development and software engineering because they allow programmers and computer programmers to simulate the behaviour of an individual's ability to make decisions and perform actions based on those decisions. Conditional statements are used by developers and software technicians to enable a device to simulate the behaviour of an effect in order to make decisions and perform actions based on those decisions.

Conditional expressions are a programming language feature that provides programmers with tools and features that they may alter in order to put a machine to productive use.

Allow me to explain the different sorts of conditional statements for the benefit of clarity. Please remember that all conditionals return a bool, which means that they are either true or false.

Conditional expressions are used in a variety of programming languages to advise the computer on which choice to make in response to a set of circumstances. According to the function the developer has in mind, these choices are made only if the post criteria are all either true or untrue, at which point the decision is made.

Conditional expression syntax is included in all programming languages.

4.2: If-Else Condition

Using C's if-else statement, you may conduct specified actions depending on a predefined condition. If the supplied condition is met, the actions stated in the if block is carried out.

The if-else statement lets you make a choice based on the circumstances that have been specified. If the provided condition is met, the statements included within the body of the logical 'if' are performed, whilst the statements contained within the body of the logical 'otherwise' are not executed. Likewise, if the criteria are fulfilled, the statements included within the content of the if statement is disregarded, and the statements contained within the 'otherwise' statement are performed.

Take the following abc expression as an example to have a better grasp of the principle:

1. If indeed the 'abc expression' is true, the following statements are performed: statements within the body of 'if' are executed, statements within the body of otherwise are disregarded

2. If indeed the 'abc expression' is false, the following sentences are performed: statements within the body of 'if' are ignored, statements within the body of else are executed

The if-else statement, in its most basic form, regulates the flow of a program and is hence referred to as the Control Flow statement.

Pros:

- The if-else statement aids us in making decisions in programming and executing the appropriate computer code.

- It also aids in the debugging of software.

Cons:

- If-else statements have the disadvantage of increasing the number of code paths that must be examined.

- When there are a large number of if statements, the code may become illegible and complicated; in these circumstances, the Switch case statement is used.

The following is a list of C language if statements

- If statement

- If-else statement

- If else-if ladder

- Nested if

If

It is possible to take certain actions in response to the validity of a condition by using the if statement. It's most useful when dealing with a variety of situations that call for a variety of actions to be taken. The if statement's syntax is seen in the following example.

```
if(expression){

//code inserted here

}
```

Example 1: To find out if a number entered is even

```
#include<stdio.h>

int main(){

int number=0;

printf("Enter a number:");

scanf("%d",&number);

if(number%2==0){

printf("%d is even number",number);

}
```

```c
return 0;

}
```

Output

```
C:\Windows\system32\cmd.exe
Enter a number:6
6 is even number
Press any key to continue . . .
```

Example 2: To find the largest of three variables.

```c
#include <stdio.h>

int main()

{

    int a, b, c;

     printf("Enter three numbers");

    scanf("%d %d %d",&a,&b,&c);

    if(a>b && a>c)   // if a>b and a>c

    {

        printf("%d is largest",a);

    }

    if(b>a  && b > c)  //if b>a and b>c

    {
```

```c
        printf("%d is largest",b);

}

if(c>a && c>b)   //if c>a and c>b

{

    printf("%d is largest",c);

}

if(a == b && a == c)   // if all are equal

{

    printf("All are equal");

}

}
```

Output:

```
C:\Windows\system32\cmd.exe
Enter three numbers4
2
1
4 is largest
Press any key to continue . . .
```

If-Else

It is possible to conduct two actions for one condition using the if-else expression. As an extension of the if-else statement, the if-else statement may be used for both the correctness and the incorrectness of a given condition, respectively. The if and else blocks cannot be run simultaneously in this case. Since every if condition triggers an otherwise scenario, using an if-else statement is almost always preferable.

The if-else statement's syntax is seen in the following example.

if(expression){

//code to be executed if the condition is true

}else{

//code to be executed if the condition is false

}

Example 3:

#include<stdio.h>

int main(){

int number=0;

printf("enter a number:");

scanf("%d",&number);

if(number%2==0){

```c
printf("%d is even number",number);

}

else{

printf("%d is odd number",number);

}

return 0;

}
```

Output:

```
C:\Windows\system32\cmd.exe
enter a number:45
45 is odd number
Press any key to continue . . .
```

Example 4: Check if you can pay taxes

```c
#include <stdio.h>

int main()

{

    int age;

    printf("Enter age: ");

    scanf("%d",&age);

    if(age>=18)

    {
```

```
        printf("You are able and must pay.");

    }

    else

    {

        printf("Sorry, you can't pay any taxes.");

    }

}
```

Output:

```
C:\Windows\system32\cmd.exe
Enter age: 34
You are able and must to pay.
Press any key to continue . . .
```

Ladder, If Else-If

This statement is an extension of the previous if-else statement, which is called the if-else-if ladder statement. It is employed in situations when a large number of instances must be done under a variety of diverse settings. An if-else-if ladder statement is used to test whether or not a given condition is true. If one of the conditions is true, the declarations defined in the if frame will be executed. If another condition is true, the comments characterized in the else square will be executed. If no condition is true, the observations defined in the else block will be executed. There are a variety of else-if blocks that may

be used. Similar to the switch case statement, the default is run rather than an else block because none of the cases is matched by the default condition.

```
if(condition1){

//code to be executed if condition1 is true

}else if(condition2){

//code to be executed if condition2 is true

}

else if(condition3){

//code to be executed if condition3 is true

}
```

...

else{

//code to be executed if all the conditions are false

}

Example 5:

```c
#include<stdio.h>

int main(){

int number=0;

printf("enter a number:");

scanf("%d",&number);

if(number==10){

printf("number is equals to 10");

}

else if(number==50){

printf("number is equal to 50");

}

else if(number==100){

printf("number is equal to 100");

}
```

```c
else{

printf("number is not equal to 10, 50 or 100");

}

return 0;

}
```

Output:

```
C:\Windows\system32\cmd.exe
enter a number:45
number is not equal to 10, 50 or 100
Press any key to continue . . .
```

Example 6: Grade Assigner

```c
#include <stdio.h>

int main()

{

    int marks;

    printf("Enter your marks?");

    scanf("%d",&marks);

    if(marks > 85 && marks <= 100)

    {

        printf("Congrats ! you scored grade A ...");

    }
```

```c
else if (marks > 60 && marks <= 85)

{

    printf("You scored grade B + ...");

}

else if (marks > 40 && marks <= 60)

{

    printf("You scored grade B ...");

}

else if (marks > 30 && marks <= 40)

{

    printf("You scored grade C ...");

}

else

{

    printf("Sorry you failed ...");

}

}
```

Output:

```
C:\Windows\system32\cmd.exe
Enter your marks?87
Congrats ! you scored grade A ...
Press any key to continue . . .
```

4.3: Switch Condition

When using the conditional statements in C, we can perform multiple operations for each of the distinct combinations of a single value called the switch variable. The switch statement is an alternative to the if-else-if ladder statement, and it allows us to perform multiple operations for each of the distinct combinations of a single value called the switch variable. For a single variable, we may construct many statements in several cases again for various values of the same variable in this section.

Pros:

1. It is less difficult to understand than the comparable if-else statement.

2. Possibility of more rapid execution.

3. It is less difficult to debug.

4. It is less difficult to maintain.

5. A succession of "if-else" statements results in deep nesting, which makes compilation more difficult to complete, specifically in naturally given codes.

6. The destination may be calculated by searching it in a database, which is more efficient than the comparable if-else expression.

7. Additionally, since it is often accomplished by utilizing an indexed branch table, an optimized version may be far quicker than the if-else expressions in terms of execution time.

Cons:

1. Does not work for floats, strings, or other types of data.

2. Doesn't work when the circumstances are varied.

3. It is not compatible with range (unless explicitly enumerated)

4. In reality, switch/case lines are a common cause of issues among even computer engineers when built with collapse as the default route. This is due to the "break" is nearly always the intended path but just not the default behaviour of the switch/case statement.

The following is the syntax for the switch statement in the C programming language:

```c
switch(expression){

case value1:

//code to be executed;

break; //optional

case value2:

//code to be executed;

break; //optional

......

default:

code to be executed if all cases are not matched;

}
```

The following are the rules for using the switch statement in the C programming language:

1. The switch phrase will be in the form character or integer.

2. In the switch situation, the break statement is not required. If no breakpoint is detected in the instance, all of the cases that are present following the matched case will be performed. A C switch statement's state transition is referred to as a fall-through state transition.

3. In the switch statement, the case values could only be utilized within the switch clause.

4. Integer or character constants must be used as the case value in the first place.

Please use the following examples to help you better grasp what I'm saying. We are in work with the assumption that the following variables exist:

int x,y,z;

char a,b;

float f;

Valid Switch	Invalid Switch	Valid Case	Invalid Case
switch(x)	switch(f)	case 3;	case 2.5;
switch(func(x,y))	-	case 'x'>'y';	case 1,2,3;
switch(x>y)	switch(x+2.5)	case 'a';	case x;
switch(a+b-2)	-	case 1+2;	case x+2;

The Operation of the Switch Case

It is first necessary to evaluate the integer phrase supplied in the switch statement. This amount is equivalent one by one to the fixed values that have been provided in each of the circumstances. If a match is discovered, then all of the statements stated in that case, as well as all of the cases that follow that case, along with the default declaration, are performed. There can be no two situations with the same values. If the selected case includes a debugging tool, then all of the cases that follow it will be ignored, and control will be passed via the switch to the next case. If this is not the case, all of the cases that follow the match case will be performed.

Here is a basic example of a switch statement in the C programming language:

```
#include<stdio.h>

int main(){

int number=0;

printf("enter a number:");

scanf("%d",&number);

switch(number){

case 10:

printf("number is equals to 10");
```

```c
break;

case 50:

printf("number is equal to 50");

break;

case 100:

printf("number is equal to 100");

break;

default:

printf("number is not equal to 10, 50 or 100");

}

return 0;

}
```

Output:

Example 1: Hi Printing

```c
#include <stdio.h>

int main()
```

```c
{
    int x = 10, y = 5;

    switch(x>y && x+y>0)

    {
        case 1:
        printf("hi");
        break;
        case 0:
        printf("bye");
        break;
        default:
        printf(" Hello bye ");
    }


}
```

Output:

```
C:\Windows\system32\cmd.exe
hi
Press any key to continue . . .
```

C switch conditional statements are fall-through

The switch declaration in the C programming language falls through, which means that if you're not using a break statement inside the switch case, all of the instances after the matched case will be performed.

Example 2: Using the 10,50,100 code

```
#include<stdio.h>

int main(){

int number=0;

printf("enter a number:");

scanf("%d",&number);

switch(number){

case 10:

printf("number is equal to 10\n");

case 50:

printf("number is equal to 50\n");

case 100:

printf("number is equal to 100\n");
```

default:

printf("number is not equal to 10, 50 or 100");

}

return 0;

}

Output:

```
C:\Windows\system32\cmd.exe
enter a number:10
number is equal to 10
number is equal to 50
number is equal to 100
number is not equal to 10, 50 or 100
Press any key to continue . . .
```

```
C:\Windows\system32\cmd.exe
enter a number:50
number is equal to 50
number is equal to 100
number is not equal to 10, 50 or 100
Press any key to continue . . .
```

Switch case statements that are nested

Within a switch statement, you may get as many switch statements as you would like to accomplish your goal. Nesting switch-case statements are a sort of statement that is used in this manner.

Example 3: Nested Switch

#include <stdio.h>

```c
int main () {

    int i = 10;

    int j = 20;

    switch(i) {

        case 10:
            printf("the value of i evaluated in outer switch: %d\n",i);
        case 20:
            switch(j) {
                case 20:
                    printf("The value of j evaluated in nested switch: %d\n",j);
            }
    }

    printf("Exact value of i is : %d\n", i );
    printf("Exact value of j is : %d\n", j );
```

return 0;

}

Output:

```
C:\Windows\system32\cmd.exe
the value of i evaluated in outer switch: 10
The value of j evaluated in nested switch: 20
Exact value of i is : 10
Exact value of j is : 20

Press any key to continue . . .
```

4.4: If-Else vs. Switch Conditions

There is a resemblance between if-else and switch

For both if-else and switch statements serve as decision-making statements in the program. The term "decision-making statements" refers to the fact that the result of the phrase will determine which declarations are to be carried out.

Distinctions between an if-else and a switch statement

Hereunder are the distinctions between an if-else statement and a switch statement:

1. **Evaluation**

If-else

An if-else statement may assess practically any form of data, including integers, floating-point numbers, characters, pointers, and Boolean values, among others.

Switch

A switch statement may be used to assess perhaps an integer or a string of characters.

2. Editing

If-else

It is difficult to make changes to an 'if-else' statement since removing the 'else' statement would cause chaos with the rest of the code.

Switch

When compared to the 'if-else' statement, editing the switch statement is less difficult. Any cases that are removed from the switch will not interfere with the execution of the other instances that are still in the switch. Because of this, we can argue that the compound sentence is simple to edit and keep up to date.

3. Expression

If-else

The expression might be either a single phrase or a collection of phrases for numerous selections. When using this method, a value is found depending on a set of values or criteria. It tests for equality as well as logical expressions in the same way.

Switch

A single expression is included inside this block, and this expression may be either a solitary integer item or a string object. It merely tests for equality in expressions.

4. The Order in Which Events Take Place

If-else

In the case of an 'if-else' statement, depending on the situation, else the 'if' frame or the 'else' section will be performed rather than both.

Switch

Similarly, when using the 'switch' statement, each case will be processed one by one until either the break word is not found or the defaults are run.

5. Default Method of Execution

If-else

If the condition included inside the 'if' statement is not met, the else block lines will be performed by default rather than the else statement.

Switch

Default statements are executed if the phrase provided inside the switch statement does not match any of the cases. If no default statement is defined, the default statement will be executed.

6. Values

If-else

The values are determined depending on the condition supplied inside the 'if' clause. According to the value, either the 'if' or 'otherwise' block is invoked and will be performed.

Switch

The user is in charge of determining the value in this scenario. The matter will be carried out in accordance with the user's selection.

7. Speed

If-else

When there are several options, the pace at which 'if-else' statements are executed is sluggish.

Switch

A jump table is created at compile time as a result of the case values in the switch expression. This jump table determines the route to take the execution depending on the result of the expression. If we have a choice between two options, the switch statement will be executed considerably more quickly than the comparable logic of the 'if-else' expression.

8. Use

If-else

It determines whether a condition is true or untrue based on its evaluation.

Switch

A compound sentence contrasts the value of a variable with the values of many other variables. If the value matches one of the cases, the statements associated with that case will be run. Otherwise, the value will not be matched.

4.5: Loops

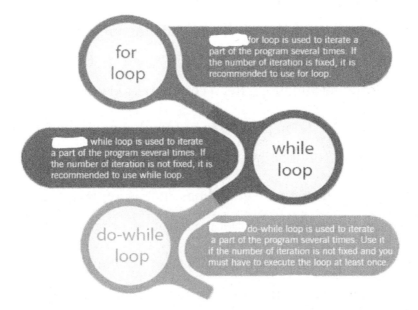

for loop is used to iterate a part of the program several times. If the number of iteration is fixed, it is recommended to use for loop.

while loop is used to iterate a part of the program several times. If the number of iteration is not fixed, it is recommended to use while loop.

do-while loop is used to iterate a part of the program several times. Use it if the number of iteration is not fixed and you must have to execute the loop at least once.

When a piece of code has to be performed several times, you may come into scenarios where this is necessary. In general, instructions are performed in a sequential manner: the first line in a code is performed first, succeeded by the next, and so on. However, there are exceptions.

Programming languages offer a variety of control structures that enable more complex execution routes to be implemented.

With the help of a loop statement, we may repeat the execution of a statement or collection of statements many times. The typical form of a loop structure in the majority of programming languages is shown in the table below.

An endless loop does not have an exit procedure that works. Consequently, the loop continues to run indefinitely till the operating system detects it and ends the program with an error or until another event happens, such as the program automatically terminating after a certain period of time.

The statement for Loop just has to be typed once, as well as the looping will be run ten times, as seen in the example below.

A loop is a collection of guidelines that is replayed until a predetermined condition is met in computer programming.

- Following the completion of an operation, such as retrieving and altering data, a condition is verified, such as determining whether a number has reached the necessary number.

- Suppose the counter does not reach the intended number, and this next instruction in the series returns to the very first command in the chain and repeats it. If the counter does not attain the optimum number, this next command in the chain returns to the first operation in the series and repeats it.

If the condition is met, the following instruction "falls through" to the next consecutive operation or branches outside of the loop, and the loop is terminated.

There are two basic kinds of loops:

1. Entry-Driven Loops: In this sort of loop, the test circumstance is checked prior to accessing the loop body. The loop body is then tested once the test condition is passed. Loops with entrance-controlled entry are the For Loop and the While Loop.

2. Exit Driven Loops: In this form of a loop, the testing test expression is evaluated or assessed at the end of the loop body, which is called an exit-controlled loop. The looping content will thus be executed at least once, regardless of whether the make it apparent is true or untrue in the conditional statement. Exit-controlled loops are represented by the do-while loop.

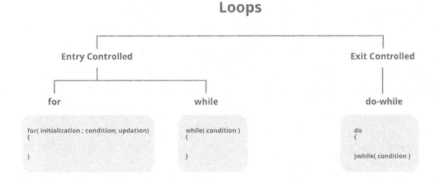

1. **For Loop**

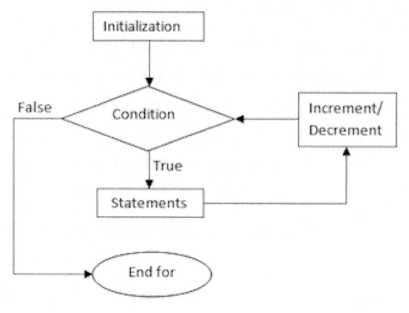

fig: Flowchart for for loop

It is possible to build a for loop, which is a control flow statement structure that will be run a particular number of times. The loop allows us to do an n series of steps in a single line by grouping them together.

The for loop is controlled by a loop variable, which is defined as follows: Then verify whether the value of this loop parameter is below or more than the value of the counter variable. If the statement is correct, the body of the loop is run, and the loop variables are modified automatically. The steps are repeated until the exit condition is reached.

Initialization Expression: We must initialize the loop count to a certain number in this affirmation. as an illustration: int i = 1;

Test Statement: In this expression, we must put the condition under scrutiny. The body of the loop will be completed, and we will go on to the update expression if the given condition is true; otherwise, we will leave the for loop and return. As an illustration: I am equal to 10;

Update Expression: After the loop body has been executed, this expression increases or decreases the value of the loop variable by a specified amount. as an illustration: i++;

Syntax:

for (initialization expr; test expr; update expr)

{

    // body of the loop

    // statements we want to execute

}

Example 1: Print Hello World

// C program to illustrate for loop

#include <stdio.h>

```c
int main()

{

    int i=0;


    for (i = 1; i <= 10; i++)

    {

        printf( "Hello World\n");

    }


    return 0;

}
```

Output:

Nested for Loop

When you include a for loop within the other loop, it is called a nested for loop. The inner loop runs entirely anytime the outside loop executes.

Example 2: Prime numbers between 2 and 100

```c
#include <stdio.h>

int main () {

   /* local variable definition */
   int i, j;
   for(i = 2; i<100; i++)
     for(j = 2; j <= (i/j); j++)
     if(!(i%j)) break; // if factor found, not prime
     if(j > (i/j)) printf("%d is prime\n", i);
   }
   return 0;
}
```

Output:

```
C:\Windows\system32\cmd.exe
2 is prime
3 is prime
5 is prime
7 is prime
11 is prime
13 is prime
17 is prime
19 is prime
23 is prime
29 is prime
31 is prime
37 is prime
41 is prime
43 is prime
47 is prime
53 is prime
59 is prime
61 is prime
67 is prime
71 is prime
73 is prime
79 is prime
83 is prime
89 is prime
97 is prime
```

2. While Loop

A pre-tested loop is another name for a while loop. With a while loop, a section of code may be run several times depending on whether a certain boolean condition is true or false. It's possible to see it as a recursive if statement. When the number of cycles isn't known ahead of time, the while loop is often employed.

What's the deal with while loops?

- The testExpression within the parenthesis is evaluated by the while loop ().

- The while loop's body executes any statements that are true if the testExpression variable is true. A second time, testExpression is put to the test.

- Once testExpression is judged to be false, the procedure repeats itself until it does.

- It stops if testExpression returns false (ends).

Syntax:

```
while (testExpression) {

  // the body of the loop

}
```

Example 3:

```
// Print numbers from 1 to 5


#include <stdio.h>

int main() {

  int i = 1;


  while (i <= 5) {

  printf("%d\n", i);

  ++i;

}
```

```
    return 0;

}
```

Output:

3. Do-While Loop

With one notable exception, the do..while loop resembles the while loop. At least one iteration of the do...while the loop's body is performed. The test expression can only be evaluated after that.

What's the deal with do..while loops?

- Execution of the loop's body occurs once. Only then will the testExpression be tested.

- There is a second evaluation of testExpression if testExpression equals valid, and then the loop body is run twice.

- This cycle continues until testExpression is determined to be incorrect.

- The loop comes to an end if testExpression returns false.

Syntax:

```
{
  // the body of the loop
}
while (testExpression);
```

Example 4:

```
// Program to add numbers until the user enters zero


#include <stdio.h>
int main() {
  double number, sum = 0;


  // the body of the loop is executed at least once
  do {
    printf("Enter a number: ");
    scanf("%lf", &number);
    sum += number;
  }
```

```c
while(number != 0.0);



printf("Sum = %.2lf",sum);



return 0;

}
```

Output:

```
C:\Windows\system32\cmd.exe
Enter a number: 6
Enter a number: 3
Enter a number: 2
Enter a number: 5
Enter a number: 3
Enter a number: 2
Enter a number: 7
Enter a number: 8
Enter a number: 0
Sum = 36.00
Press any key to continue . . .
```

4. Infinite Loop

When a piece of code does not have a functioning exit, it is known as an infinite loop (endless loop). This happens when a predicate always returns true. This is usually a mistake.

Example 5:

```c
// C program to demonstrate infinite loops

// using for and while

// Uncomment the sections to see the output
```

```c
#include <stdio.h>

int main ()
{
    int i;

    // This is an infinite for loop as the condition
    // expression is blank
    for ( ; ; )
    {
    printf("This loop will run forever.\n");
    }

    // This is an infinite for loop as the condition
    // given in while loop will keep repeating infinitely
    /*
    while (i != 0)
    {
```

```c
        i-- ;

    printf( "This loop will run forever.\n");

}
*/


// This is an infinite for loop as the condition

// given in while loop is "true"

/*

while (true)

{

    printf( "This loop will run forever.\n");

}
*/

}
```

Output:

Break Keyword

When the break statement is met, the loop is instantly broken.

The syntax is:

break;

Example 6:

```
while (testExpression) {
    // codes
    if (condition to break) {
        break;
    }
    // codes
}
```

```
do {
    // codes
    if (condition to break) {
        break;
    }
    // codes
} while (testExpression);
```

```
for (init; testExpression; update) {
    // codes
    if (condition to break) {
        break;
    }
    // codes
}
```

Continue Keyword

When the continue statement is used, the loop's current iteration is skipped in favour of the next. The syntax is:

```
while (testExpression) {
    // codes
    if (testExpression) {
        continue;
    }
    // codes
}
```

```
do {
    // codes
    if (testExpression) {
        continue;
    }
    // codes
} while (testExpression);
```

```
for (init; testExpression; update) {
    // codes
    if (testExpression) {
        continue;
    }
    // codes
}
```

Chapter 5: Pointers

A pointer is changeable and contains the address of some other variable in the C programming language. This variable may be an integer, a character, an array, a procedure, or any other sort of pointer. The architecture determines the pointer's size. However, in 32-bit architecture, a pointer is two bytes in size.

Consider the following instance for defining a pointer that stores an integer's address.

Example 1:

```c
#include <stdio.h>


int main()
{
    int n = 10;

    int* p = &n; // Variable p of type pointer is pointing to the
address of the variable n of type integer.

}
```

5.1: Declaring a Pointer

The pointer may be specified using the * operator (asterisk symbol) in the C programming language. Additionally, it is referred to as an indirection pointer and is utilized to dereference a pointer.

Example 2:

```
#include <stdio.h>


int main()
{
    int* a;//pointer to int
    char* c;//pointer to char
}
```

Pointer Example 3:

Below is an illustration of how to utilize pointers to display the address and value.

Pointers in C++

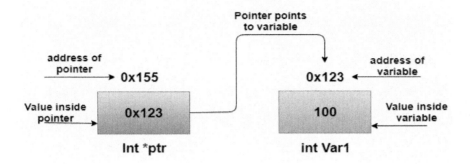

As seen above, the pointer variable holds the address of the number variable, which is 0x123. The number variable has a value of 100. However, the pointer variable ptr's address is 0x155. You may print the value of the pointer variable ptr using the * (indirection operator).

Consider the pointer example as described in the preceding illustration.

Example 4:

#include<stdio.h>

int main()

{

    int Var1 = 100;

    int* ptr;

    ptr = &Var1;//stores the address of number variable

printf("Address of p variable is %x \n", ptr); // p contains the address of the number; therefore printing p gives the address of the number.

printf("Value of p variable is %d \n", *ptr); // As you know that * is used to dereference a pointer; therefore, if you print *p, you will get the value stored at the address contained by p.

return 0;

}

Output:

```
Address of p variable is 780ff604
Value of p variable is 100
```

5.2: Pointer to Array

Example 5:

```
#include <stdio.h>

int main() {

    int x[4];

    int i;


    for (i = 0; i < 4; ++i) {

        printf("&x[%d] = %p\n", i, &x[i]);
```

```
    }


    printf("Address of array x: %p\n", x);


    return 0;

}
```

Output:

```
&x[0] = 0000005662EFF8A8
&x[1] = 0000005662EFF8AC
&x[2] = 0000005662EFF8B0
&x[3] = 0000005662EFF8B4
Address of array x: 0000005662EFF8A8
```

5.3: Pointer to a Function

Example 6:

```
#include <stdio.h>

void swap(int* n1, int* n2);


int main()

{

    int num1 = 5, num2 = 10;
```

```c
    // address of num1 and num2 is passed

    swap(&num1, &num2);


    printf("num1 = %d\n", num1);

    printf("num2 = %d\n", num2);

    return 0;
}


void swap(int* n1, int* n2)
{
    int temp;

    temp = *n1;

    *n1 = *n2;

    *n2 = temp;
}
```

Output:

```
num1 = 10
num2 = 5
```

5.3: Pointer to Structure

Example 7:

```c
#include <stdio.h>

struct person
{
    int age;
    float weight;
};


int main()
{
    struct person* personPtr, person1;
    personPtr = &person1;

    printf("Enter age: ");
    scanf_s("%d", &personPtr->age);

    printf("Enter weight: ");
    scanf_s("%f", &personPtr->weight);
```

```
printf("Displaying:\n");

printf("Age: %d\n", personPtr->age);

printf("weight: %f", personPtr->weight);


return 0;

}
```

Output:

```
Enter age: 25
Enter weight: 48
Displaying:
Age: 25
weight: 48.000000
```

5.4: Advantages of Pointer

- A pointer simplifies code and increases efficiency; it is used to retrieve strings, trees, and other data types and is compatible with structures, arrays, and functions.

- Using the pointer, you may return several values from a function.

- It enables you to retrieve any memory address on the computer.

5.5: Usage of Pointer

There are several uses for pointers in the C programming language.

1) Dynamic memory allocation

In the C programming language, you may dynamically allocate memory by utilizing the malloc() and calloc() methods, which both employ the reference.

2) Functions, Arrays, and Structures

Pointers are extensively employed in functions, arrays, and structures in the C programming language. It simplifies the code and boosts performance.

Address Of (&) Operator:

The address returned by the operator '&' is that of a variable. However, you must use %u to show a variable's address.

Example 8:

```
#include<stdio.h>

int main()
{
    int Var1 = 100;
```

printf("value of number is %d, address of number is %u\n", Var1, &Var1);

    return 0;

}

Output:

```
value of number is 100, address of number is 2066740740
```

NULL Pointer:

The NULL pointer is a pointer that is not allocated any value other than NULL. If there is no address to provide in the pointer at the point of declaration, you may use NULL. It will create a more effective strategy.

Example 9:

#include<stdio.h>

int main()

{

    int* p = NULL;

}

The pointer's value is 0. (zero) in most libraries.

Example 10: A pointer program is used to swap two values without using the third variable.

```c
#include<stdio.h>

int main()

{

    int a = 10, b = 20, * p1 = &a, * p2 = &b;


    printf("Before swap: *p1=%d *p2=%d", *p1, *p2);

    *p1 = *p1 + *p2;

    *p2 = *p1 - *p2;

    *p1 = *p1 - *p2;

    printf("\nAfter swap: *p1=%d *p2=%d", *p1, *p2);


    return 0;

}
```

Output:

```
Before swap: *p1=10 *p2=20
After swap: *p1=20 *p2=10
```

5.5: Reading complex Pointers

Numerous factors must be considered while reading complicated pointers in C. Let us examine the associativity and precedence of the operators used to manipulate pointers.

Operator	Precedence	Associativity
(), []	1	Left to right
*, identifier	2	Right to left
Data type	3	-

You must bear in mind that, in this case.

- (): This is a bracket operative for declaring and defining a function.

- []: This operation is a subscript operator for arrays.

- *: This is a pointer-based operator.

- Identifier: This is the pointer's name. This will always be given precedence.

- Data type: The variable's data type is specified to which the pointer is pointing. Additionally, it incorporates modifiers such as signed int, long, and so on).

How to interpret the pointer: int (*p)[10]:

To interpret the pointer, it is necessary to understand that () & [] have equal priority. As a result, their associativity should be taken into account. Because associativity goes left to right, priority is given to ().

Within the bracket (), the pointer operator * and the pointer name (identifier) p are equivalent. As a result of their associativity being the right to leave, the priority is given to p, and the second priority is given to *. Assign [] the third priority since the data type takes precedence. As a result, the pointer will appear as follows.

- char -> 4

- -> 2

- p -> 1

- [10] -> 3

The pointer will be interpreted as p is a pointer to a ten-dimensional array of numbers.

Example 11:

How should the following pointer be read?

int (*p)(int(*)[2], int(*)void))

Explanation:

This pointer will be viewed as p is a pointer to a function that takes the first argument as a pointer to a two-dimensional array of numbers of size two & the 2nd parameter as a pointer to a function with a void parameter and an integer return type.

Chapter 6: Functions

6.1: About Functions

In C, you may decompose a big program into its fundamental building parts, referred to as functions. The function is composed of the collection of programming statements denoted by. Several times, a function may be called to ensure the C program's reusability and modularity. In other terms, a program is created by a collection of functions. In other programming languages, the function is referred to as a process or subroutine.

6.2: Benefits of Functions in C

Following are some of the benefits of C functions.

- You may avoid repeatedly recreating the same logic/code in software by utilizing functions.

- You may call C functions as many times as you like inside a program and from any location within the program.

- When a huge C program is broken into numerous functions, you can simply follow it.

- The primary goal of C functions is reusability.

- However, in a C program, function calls are always overhead.

6.3: Function Aspects

A C function has three distinct characteristics.

- Function declaration

The definition of a function To inform the compiler of the given function arguments and return type function, a function must be defined globally in a C program before it may be used.

Syntax:

return_type function_name (argument list);

- Function call

Anywhere in the program may invoke a function. The argument list must be the same when calling and declaring functions. You must provide the same set of functions that the function definition specifies. Invocation of a function It is possible to invoke a function just about anywhere in the program. When calling a function and declaring a function, the argument lists cannot be different from one another. We must pass the very same variety of functions as the number of functions that were defined in the function definition.

Syntax:

function_name (argument_list)

- Function definition

This section includes the actual statements that will be performed. This is the most critical component over which the function has control when it is invoked. At this point, it's worth noting that the function can return just one value. Definition of the function It consists of the actual statements that will be performed by the program. Whenever the function is invoked, the control is transferred to the most significant component of the function. It is crucial to note that the task may only return a single value at this point.

Syntax:

return_type function_name (argument list)

{function body;}

Function Syntax:

#include <stdio.h>

int main()

{

```
return_type function_name(data_type parameter...)

{

    //code to be executed

}

}
```

6.4: Types of Functions

In C programming, there are two distinct kinds of functions:

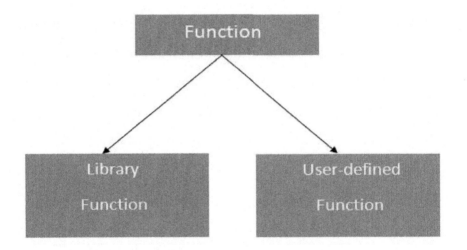

- Library Functions:

The term "library functions" refers to functions defined in C header files, like printf(), scanf(), puts(), gets(), ceil(), and floor().

- User-defined functions:

User-defined functions are functions that the C programmer creates in order to reuse them many times. It simplifies and optimizes the code of a large program.

Return Value:

A C function may not always produce any value. If the function is not required to return any value, use void as the return type. Consider a basic C function that does not return any value.

Example without return value:

```
#include <stdio.h>


int main()
{


    void hello();

    {

        printf("hello c\n");

    }

}
```

Output:

To output any value from a method, you must utilize any data type, including int, long, and char (among others). A function's return type is determined by the value that will be returned from it. Let's look at a basic C function that returns an integer value as a result of the function.

Example with return value:

```
#include <stdio.h>


int main()

{

    int get();

    {

        return 10;

    }

}
```

Because you need to return a number as a result of the preceding example, the return data type is int. If you wish to return a floating-point value (for example, 10.2, 3.1, 54.5, and so on), you must specify float as the return data type of the function in question.

Example 1:

```
#include <stdio.h>


int main()

{


    float get();

    {

        return 10.2;

    }

}
```

You must now call the function in order to get the value returned by the function.

6.5: Numerous facets of Function Invocation

Depending on the function, it may not always take any arguments. It may also not yield any useful information. The following are the four distinct features of function calls that may be derived from these facts:

- Function without return value and arguments

- Function with return value and with arguments

- Function with return value and without arguments

- Function without return value and with arguments

Example for Function without return value and argument:

Example 1:

#include <stdio.h>

void printName();

void main()

{

   printf("Hello ");

   printName();

}

void printName()

{

   printf("C Programmers\n");

}

Output:

```
Hello C Programmers
```

Example 2:

```c
#include<stdio.h>

void sum();

void main()
{
    printf("\nCalculating the sum of two numbers:");
    sum();
}

void sum()
{
    int x, y;
    printf("\nPlease enter two numbers\n");
    scanf_s("%d %d", &x, &y);
    printf("The sum is %d\n", x + y);
}
```

Output:

```
Calculating the sum of two numbers:
Please enter two numbers
7
13
The sum is 20
```

Example for Function with return value and without argument:

Example 3:

#include<stdio.h>

int sum();

void main()

{

   int result;

   printf("\nCalculating the sum of two numbers:\n");

   result = sum();

   printf("%d\n", result);

}

int sum()

{

   int x, y;

   printf("\nEnter two numbers\n");

```c
    scanf_s("%d %d", &x, &y);

    return x + y;

}
```

Output:

```
Calculating the sum of two numbers:

Enter two numbers
6
15
21
```

Example 4: Program to compute a square's area:

```c
#include<stdio.h>

int square();

int main()

{

    printf("Calculating the area of the square\n");

    float sq_area = square();

    printf("The area of the square is: %f\n", sq_area);

}

int square()

{

    float sq_side;
```

```
printf("Enter the square's side length in meters: ");

scanf_s("%f", &sq_side);

return sq_side * sq_side;
}
```

Output:

```
Calculating the area of the square
Enter the square's side length in meters: 15
The area of the square is: 225.000000
```

Example for Function without return value and with an argument:

Example 5:

```
#include<stdio.h>

void sum(int, int);

void main()
{
    int x, y, result;

    printf("\nCalculating the sum of two numbers:");

    printf("\nPlease enter two numbers:");

    scanf_s("%d %d", &x, &y);

    sum(x, y);
```

```
}

void sum(int x, int y)

{

    printf("The sum is %d\n", x + y);

}
```

Output:

```
Calculating the sum of two numbers:
Please enter two numbers:23
5
The sum is 28
```

Example 6: Program to find the average of five numbers.

```
#include<stdio.h>

void average(int, int, int, int, int);

void main()

{

    int a1, a2, a3, a4, a5;

    printf("\nCalculating the average of five numbers:");

    printf("\nEnter five numbers:");

    scanf_s("%d %d %d %d %d", &a1, &a2, &a3, &a4, &a5);

    average(a1, a2, a3, a4, a5);

}
```

```c
void average(int a1, int a2, int a3, int a4, int a5)

{

    float avg;

    avg = (a1 + a2 + a3 + a4 + a5) / 5;

    printf("The average of the five given numbers are: %f\n", avg);

}
```

Output:

```
Calculating the average of five numbers:
Enter five numbers:15
25
35
45
55
The average of the five given numbers are: 35.000000
```

Example for Function with return value and argument:

Example 7:

```c
#include<stdio.h>

int sum(int, int);

void main()

{

    int x, y, result;

    printf("\nCalculating the sum of two numbers:");
```

```c
    printf("\nPlease enter two numbers:");

    scanf_s("%d %d", &x, &y);

    result = sum(x, y);

    printf("The sum is : %d\n", result);

}

int sum(int x, int y)

{

    return x + y;

}
```

Output:

```
Calculating the sum of two numbers:
Please enter two numbers:3
7
The sum is : 10
```

Example 8: Program to verify whether a number is even or odd

```c
#include<stdio.h>

int even_odd(int);

void main()

{

    int n, flag = 0;

    printf("\nChecking whether a number is even or odd");
```

185

```c
    printf("\nPlease enter a number: ");

    scanf_s("%d", &n);

    flag = even_odd(n);

    if (flag == 0)

    {

        printf("The number is odd\n");

    }

    else

    {

        printf("The number is even\n");

    }

}

int even_odd(int n)

{

    if (n % 2 == 0)

    {

        return 1;

    }

    else
```

```
    {

        return 0;

    }

}
```

Output:

```
Checking whether a number is even or odd
Please enter a number: 9
The number is odd
```

C Library Functions:

Those built-in functions in C that are gathered and stored in a central location called the library are referred to as library functions. Such functions are employed to carry out a variety of specialized processes. In this case, the printf library function is used to print something on the console. Compiler designers build the library functions that are used by the compilers. Almost all of the functions in the C standard library are specified inside the various header files, which are stored with the extension .h. For our application to be able to utilize the library functions specified in these header files, you should incorporate these header files inside it. Consider the following example: in order to make use of library functions like printf/scanf, you should incorporate the header file stdio.h in our program. The header file Stdio.h includes all library functions related to standard input/output.

Given below is a list of the most often seen header files.

- stdio.h: This file is a basic input/output header file for the program. It includes all of the library functions related to standard input and output.

- setjmp.h: All of the jump routines are included inside this file.

- conio.h: This file contains the header information for console input and output.

- stdlib.h: This header file includes all of the generic library functions, such as

- string.h: Gets(), puts(), and other string-related library methods are all included in this package.

- malloc(), calloc(), exit(), and so on. It is located in the lib directory.

- time.h: This header file includes all of the functions that are connected to time.

- ctype.h: This header file provides all of the functions that deal with characters.

- math.h: These functions, such as sqrt(), pow(), and other arithmetic operations-related functions, are included inside this header file.

- assert.h: This file includes routines for doing diagnostics.

- stdarg.h: This header file contains the definitions for the variable argument functions.

- locale.h: This file includes functions that are specific to a certain locale.

- errno.h: This file includes routines for dealing with errors.

- signal.h: This header file contains the definitions for all of the signal-handling routines.

Chapter 7: Pre-processor

7.1: About Pre-processor

The C processor is a microprocessor used by the C compiler to alter your program before it is compiled. The C compiler automatically invokes it. This program is a phrase processor because it enables you to create macros and short abbreviations for lengthier structures.

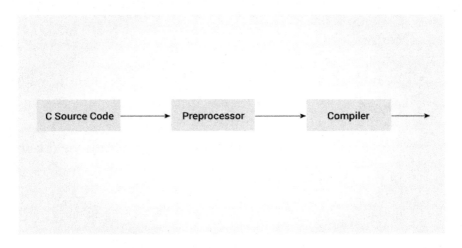

The C preprocessor offers four distinct facilities you may utilize in whatever way you see appropriate. These are as follows:

- Including header files in the package are files containing declarations that may be imported into your application as needed.

- Expansion at the macro level. Macros, which are acronyms for arbitrary bits of C code, may be defined, and then the C processor will swap the macros with the definitions of the macros throughout the program.

- Conditional compilation is a kind of compilation in which one or more conditions are met. You may include or omit program portions based on various circumstances using specific preprocessing directives.

- Line control is a kind of command. Use line command to tell the compiler where every other source line originated if you're using software to merge or rearrange compiled code into an initial file that will later be generated.

Some aspects of C preprocessors differ from one another. This document contains information about the GNU C processor, the C Compatible Compilation Coprocessor. The GNU C preprocessing is a collection of the functionality provided by the ANSI Standard C preprocessor.

Preprocessing is a processor that enables you to design abbreviations for lengthy constructions that may be used in the program instead of many lines of code to a smaller number of code lines, which saves time. In C, the compressor is not a compiler component; rather, it is a separate program used to alter code before it is built. This is also denoted as a macro processor since it assists you in defining code in short names, which are referred to as macros. Preprocessors in C give a few instructions that begin with the letter #. (Hash symbol). These preprocessing directives comprise a collection of statements that are combined into a single macro used at the start of the event so that it may be used any bunch of times throughout the program.

7.2: Pre-processor Directives

Most preprocessor features are only available if you explicitly request their usage using preprocessing directives.

It is possible to include preprocessing instructions in your program by including lines in your program that begin with '#.' The '#' character is accompanied by an identifier, the directive's name. For example, the directive '#define' is responsible for defining a macro. Additionally, whitespace is permitted before and after the '#.'

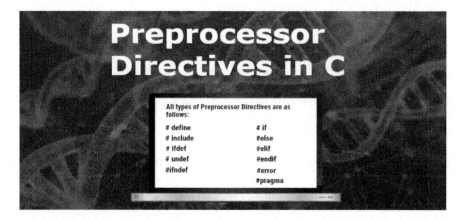

The list of permissible directive names is limited in number. There are no new preprocessing directives that programs may define.

Some directive names need the inclusion of arguments; these arguments constitute the remainder of the rule line and must be isolated from the rule name by whitespace. In the case of '#define,' it is necessary to provide the macro's name and the desired extension of the macro. See the section on Simple Macros for further information.

Normal conditions do not allow a preprocessing directive to be longer than one line. It is possible to separate it aesthetically using Backslash-Newline, although this does not influence the meaning of the character. Comments containing Newlines may also break up a directive into many lines, but the arguments are converted to Spaces even before parsing and implementing the directive. There is just one place where a meaningful Newline may appear in a preprocessing directive: inside a string constant or a character constant. Note that almost all C compilers that may be deployed to the outputs from the preprocessing do not accept word or character constants that include Newlines as parameters.

#define

#define AGE 50

#ifdef

#ifdef SOLARIS

#ifndef

#ifndef WINDOWS

#warning

#warning Non-critical error found

#error

#error Windows is an unsupported platform

The '#' and the guideline name can't be derived from a macro expansion. For example, if the word 'foo' is specified as a macro that expands to the word 'define,' this does not imply that the preprocessing directive '#foo' is legal.

A developer writes a C program, and the program checks to see whether any preprocessor directives are accessible before continuing. The act event of the preprocessor will be performed if it is available; otherwise, the compiler will build the object code. The linker will next carry out the instructions in the code. If no preprocessor commands are provided, the program will be passed to the compiler. The compiler will generate the object code, and the linker will execute the code after that.

7.3: Headers files

A header file is a file that encompasses C directives and macro definitions that are shared amongst various source files. When you use the C preprocessor directive '#include' in your program, you request that a header file be included in your program. The inheritance includes one main program in that other header file (or vice versa).

Header files are supporting files for your C program that include definitions of different functions and their related variables, which must be exported into your C program with the assistance of the preprocessor #include a command for your C program to operate properly. All header files have the extension '.h,' which includes C function declarations and macro definitions. The header files may be requested by using the preprocessor command #include, or in other words, they can be requested. The studio .h header file is the usual header file, including the C compiler. Incorporating a header file implies that the content of the header file will be used in your source program programming in C or C++ applications. A basic approach keeps all macros, environment variables, constant, and other code ideas in the header files rather than in the basic code itself.

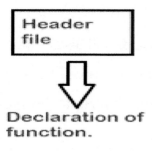

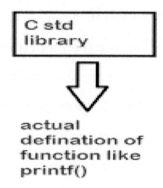

7.4: Uses of header files

Header files serve two kinds of tenacities.

- The interfaces to various portions of the operating system are characterized in system header files. You have them with your program to provide the definitions and declare that you will need to invoke system functions and libraries.

- In your program's header files, you'll see declarations for interfaces that connect the various source files. When you have a collection of related and macro definitions required in many basis files, it is a good impression to create a header file for each of those files.

Including a header file achieves the same consequences as copying the data type into each source code that requires it in the C compilation process. On the other hand, such copying would've been time-consuming and error-prone. All associated declarations are included in a single file when using a header file. They may be modified in a single location if needed, and applications that include header files will utilize the new edition when they are recompiled the next time. The header file removes the time-consuming task of locating and modifying all of the copies, and the danger was that failing to locate one copy would result in errors across the program.

The standard approach is to name header files with a '.h' suffix at the end. Make an effort to avoid using odd characters in header file names since this would impair portability.

#Input/Output functions

stdio.h

#Console Input/Output functions

conio.h

#General utility functions

stdlib.h

#Mathematics functions

math.h

#String functions

string.h

#Character handling functions

type.h

#Date and time functions

time.h

#Limits of float types

float.h

Pre-Existing Files

These files are the ones that are already present in the C compiler; all we have to do is import them anytime we wish to utilize them. As an example, #include Filename.h>

User-Defined Files

"#include" is used when users wish to specify their header, which can be easily imported by using the "#include" command. For example, #include "Filename. h" would be appropriate.

In conclusion, these are the 2 techniques through which we may include the header file in our application. The preprocessor directive "#include," for example, is simply responsible for informing the translator that the header file must be evaluated before the main compilation and that it must include all of the essential functionalities for the program to run. After searching for a document in the current working directory and locating it, the user-defined data type calls the file from inside the application.

```c
int main()

{

int num1 = 25;

int num2 = 3;

int t=0, m=0;

t = sqrt(num1);

m = pow(t, num2);

printf("t = %d\n ", t);

printf("m = %d ", m);

return

0;

}
```

Output:

t = 5

m = 125

Using the pow () routines, we could compute the square root of 25 and then multiply it by three to get 5 to the power of three. We utilized two header files in the previous program, # including the studio. H>, and #include math. H>, to conduct different mathematical operations.

7.5: Macro Preprocessor

A macro is a kind of abbreviation that you may create once and then use again and again and again. There are several complex aspects of macros in the C preprocessor, all of which are explained here. Simple macros always increase in the same manner, regardless of the context. Macros that take parameters that are replaced into the macro-operation are argument macros. Predefined macros are those that have been predefined and seem to be accessible. Trinification is the process of converting macro parameters into string constants. Concatenation is the process of creating tokens from pieces taken from macro parameters. Undefining a macro is the act of removing it from its definition. Changing the definition of a macro is referred to as redefining. Pitfalls of Macroeconomics: For the uninitiated, macroeconomics may be confusing.

_ DATE_ # represents the current date in "MMM DD YYYY" format.

TIME #represents the current time in "HH:MM: SS" format.

FILE #represents the current file name.

LINE #represents the current line number.

STDC #The value 1 indicates that the compiler is compliant with the ANSI specification.

As previously discussed, macros are a type of code that contains a set of assertions that perform a specific task or logic that wants to be used multiple times throughout the program. When this logic is required, we can simply declare the specified macro in the program and call it whenever the logic is required to be executed throughout the program. If a compiler detects this prefix name in a program, the compiler substitutes the macro term with a piece of code declared at the program's start. The # define directive is used to declare the name of the macro.

#include

MAX 8 int main #define MAX 8 int ()

{

Printf ("To print the digits using the macro definition"):

For each (int I = 0; I MAX; i++) iteration of the conditional expression

{

printing (" percent dn,i); printf(" percent dn",i); printing

}

Observe that we have created a macro with the name "MAX" and a value of 8. This is shown in the program above. This signifies that the software uses a macro term to print the figures up to the macro value specified at the beginning of the program's code.

There are two sorts of macros in C: global and local. Macros behave similarly to objects and functions. A symbolic constant is used to specify identifiers in object-like macros, and a symbol represents them.

According to the accompanying diagram, the structure of the macro is as follows: You will have three components in this section:

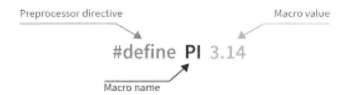

- PI - Macro Name

- 3.14 – Macro Value

- #define – Preprocessor Directive PI - Macro Value

```c
#include<stdio.h>

// This is the macro definition

#define PI 3.14

void main()

{

    // declaration and initialization of radius

    int radius = 5;

    // declaration and calculating the area

    int area = PI * (radius*radius);

    // Printing the area of the circle

    printf("Area of circle is %d", area);

}
```

Output:

The area of the round is 78.500000

7.6: Predefined macros in C

Several straightforward macros are predefined. You are free to utilize them without providing definitions for each one. Standard phrases and system-specific macros are the two types of macros that exist.

- Standard Preset: These are standard predefined macros.

- Nonstandard Predefined macros are nonstandard macros that have been predefined.

The ANSI C programming language, used in conjunction with the Program code, includes predefined macros that may be utilized in applications. Among the predefined macros is the following list, which includes the following items:

- _FILE_ this gives the current file name it will display.

- _DATE_ This macro defines the program's current date and will be displayed in "MMM DD YY" format.

- When the current time is presented in the format "HH: MM: SS," this macro also defines the current time, as specified by the macro "TIME."

- In this case, _LINE_ is a macro that specifies what line number is currently used in the program.

When the compiler produces this ANSI standard, the _STDC_ macro has an ANSI standard value of 1, indicating that it conforms to the standard.

```
#include<stdio.h>

int main()

{
```

```c
printf("Below are a few of preset macros that are often used in C:n");

printf("This will print the current File name: percent sn", __DATE__);

printf("This will print the current Time: percent sn", __TIME__);

printf("This will print the current File name: percent sn", __DATE__);

printf("This will print the current Time: percent sn", TIME );
return 0;

}
```

It is explained that when the compiler produces code that conforms to the ANSI standard, the macro STDC is set to a value of 1, indicating that the code adheres to the standard. The program provided in the example demonstrates the use of some pre-defined macros in C. For instance, the DATE macro is used to print the current date, and the TIME macro is used to print the current time. The program also attempts to print a macro called "TIME," which is not a pre-defined macro and will result in a compilation error. Overall, the program serves as an introduction to the concept of macros and how they can be used in C programming.

7.7: Conditionals

A conditional directive allows a part of the program to be ignored during compilation on some conditions in a macro processor. A conditional may verify whether or not an arithmetic phrase or a name is declared as a macro in the C preprocessor meets the criteria.

Even though a precondition in the C preprocessor is similar in some respects to an 'if' statement in C, it is critical to grasp the differences between them. The condition in an 'if' statement is evaluated during your program's execution. It aims to let your the program acts differently from one run to the next based on the operational data given.

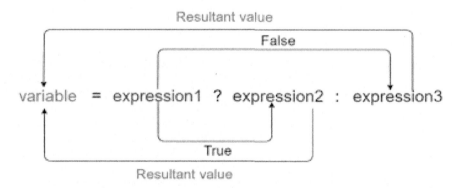

The condition in a conditional preprocessing directive is tested when your program is compiled. Its purpose is to allow different codes to be included in the program depending on the situation at compilation.

- Uses: What are conditionals for?

- Syntax: How conditionals are written.

- Deletion: Making code into a comment.

- Macros: Why conditionals are used with macros.

- Assertions: How and why to use assertions.

- Errors: Detecting inconsistent compilation parameters.

Summarizing conditionals as

- Making choices in a program may be accomplished in one of three ways. The first method involves using the

  if-else statement, the second method involves using conditional operators, and the third method involves using the switch statement.

- The standard range of the if clause is simply the following sentence, which is the most restrictive. So, to perform more than one line, they must be placed in a couple of braces.

- It is not always necessary for an if block to be coupled with another clause.

- On the other hand, an else block is always connected with an if expression.

- Once it is determined that the output of an if-else ladder can only be one of two possible outcomes, the ladders should be replaced by an else-if clause or by using logical operators.

- The binary operators && and || are used, while the unary operator ! Is used.

- The A-C test expression is evaluated using zero and non-zero values for each test expression. An integer with a zero value is regarded as false, whereas an integer with a value greater than zero is deemed true.

- Assignment statements used in conjunction with conditional operators must be contained inside a pair of parentheses.

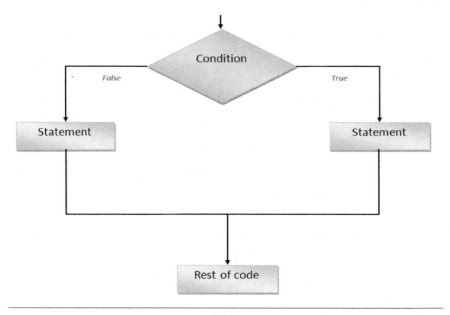

7.8: Summary

Chapter 7 discusses the pre-processor in C programming. The pre-processor is a program that allows programmers to create macros and abbreviations for longer structures in their programs. The pre-processor offers facilities for including header files, expanding macros, conditional compilation, and line control. Pre-processing directives begin with the hash symbol, and programmers can use these directives to request the pre-processor to perform various tasks. Header files contain C directives and macro definitions that are shared amongst various source files, and programmers can use the preprocessor directive #include to include header files in their programs. The chapter discusses the uses of header files, including defining the interfaces to various parts of the operating system and keeping macros and other code ideas in separate files rather than in the main code.

Chapter 8: Memory Manipulation

8.1: About Memory Manipulation

As a general rule, memory allocations run computer programs and services to reserve partial or whole amounts of physical or virtual memory on a computer; this process is called memory allocation. Essentially, this is a physical function, and it is accomplished via operational systems and software programs to manage memory. There are two types of retention allocations: static and dynamic. In the C language, we see memory allocation, which is the method of allocating memory while composing the C program, which means recollection is allocated at compile-time, and static memory allocation, which is the process of allocating remembrance during run time.

Memory allocation may be defined as " assigning memory sections to programs inside a program's execution environment. This is done to free up memory to save variables or objects of classes and structures, respectively. Whenever variables are declared, for example, the operating system generates blocks for them, which may then be accessed by defining the corresponding objects in the operating system.

C interacts with memory in three ways: automatically, statically, or dynamically. It maintains memory with methods such as realloc() and malloc() (). Dynamic Memory Allocation in C++ uses these methods; however, the new and delete operators offer functionality identical to each other, making the process easier.

There are instances in which these operators fail to function properly, and the usage of malloc is required (). On the other hand, C programmers must depend on automated, static, or addresses. Dynamic memory allocation is often the most flexible and efficient option among the three options.

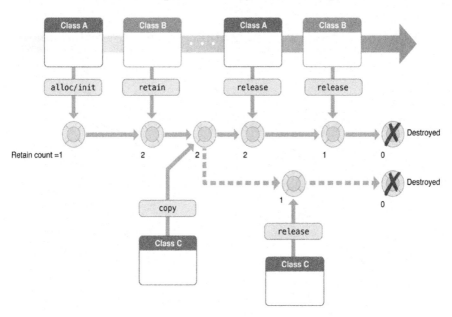

8.2: Types of Memory

Static memory:

As previously explained, static memory valuation is the process of allocating memory for data variables when computer programs are first launched. Exceptions to this form of allocation include default values, file scope variables, and variables that have been defined as static variables. This form of allocation has a disadvantage when allocating memory. We must know exactly how much memory we are allocating since this technique allocates fixed memory that cannot be altered after it has been allocated.

1. Static memory allocation has several unique characteristics. This sort of allocation assigns variables permanently, which means that the memory utilized in this kind of allocation can indeed be reused, and as a result, this kind of allocation is more inefficient. This allocation makes use of the stack to carry out the allocation operation.

void play x;

}

the first paragraph ()

{

int y; int y; int y

c[10] is an integer;

1 should be returned;

}

The variables x, y, and concern is statically allocated in the preceding program, which means that the memory for the variable data is rigorously allocated at build time. It is important to note that memory erasure is required when the values aren't being used since there will be memory leakage. The retention is inevitably released as soon as the variable's scope has expired in static memory allocation, which implies as soon as the variable's cope has expired in static memory allocation, the memory is released.

1. A variable may be defined as static either internally or externally, meaning that its value will remain constant until the conclusion of the program, and this can be accomplished by using the phrase static before the local variable. The function may have internally and externally static variables, which may be defined either into or out of the function.

void stat(void); int main()

{

for(i=1; i=3; i++) for(i=1; i=3; i++)

stat();

1 should be returned;

}

Statue of void (void)

{

N is a static integer equal to zero.

n = n+1; n = n+1;

printf("n = percent d""n", n); printf("n = percent d""n", n);

}

Dynamic memory:

The fundamental concept of Flexible Memory Allocation in C is manual memory management, which is accomplished via the use of four methods available in the C standard library. For this purpose of this, Dynamic Memory Allocation in C may be described as the process of modifying the size of data elements, such as arrays, while they are being used.

This permits memory allocation to occur during runtime rather than during compilation, as was the case with static memory space in C when compiling. Static data persists throughout the program, regardless of whether it is required. The use of dynamic memory allocation provides programmers with far more freedom in controlling the memory that has been allocated.

Memory Allocation

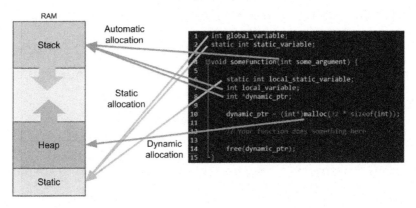

Even in automatically allocated data, it can't remain functional while being used by many functions simultaneously. Only dynamic memory allocation may be utilized across numerous scenarios due to allocating memory from the stack or free memory, a section of memory that has been specifically organized for these operations and can be used across various situations.

For manual allocation of blocks of memory from the heap, library functions (from the std lib. h header file) such as malloc() may be used, with the applications accessing these blocks via pointers returned by malloc(). When memory is no longer required or utilized, it is simply deallocated, allowing it to be utilized for other reasons in the future.

Since C is a compiled language, it has particular restrictions and constraints regarding memory management. For instance, the instructions for changing array sizes. To utterly understand dynamic memory apportionment, we must first understand an array.

Arrays can be described as gatherings of objects deposited in sequential memory positions. Consider the following scenario: an array has a length of 6 items; however, only 3 of those elements must be inserted into the array. Fundamentally, in this circumstance, the residual columns misuse RAM.

While arrays are spread evenly, half of the collection is wasted, which often occurs when generating memory during the compilation process. In addition, this kind of difficulty might occur when there are more indices than items that need to be inputted.

For example, imagine an array has 5 items, and 6 more components need to be inserted, necessitating the use of 11 indices to complete the task. When the size of an array has to be changed in these types of scenarios, dynamic memory assignment is employed to accomplish the task.

As previously noted, dynamic memory allocation is the allocation of memory throughout runtime or during the execution of a program. The C programming language uses dynamic memory allocation to perform various operations.

This type of manual memory management is made possible by four library functions in the C programming language. The following are examples of these four:

- malloc()

- free()

- calloc()

- realloc()

8.3: Dynamic Memory Allocation

The fundamental concept of Dynamic Memory Allocation in C is manual memory management, which is accomplished via the use of four methods available in the C standard library. For this purpose, Dynamic Memory Allocation in C may be described as the process of modifying the volume of data constructs such as arrays while they are being used.

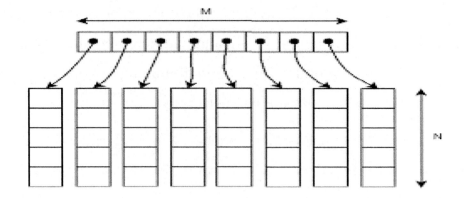

This permits memory allocation to take place during runtime rather than during compilation, as is the case with static system memory in C. Static data is stored throughout the duration of the application, regardless of whether it is required. The use of dynamic memory allocation provides programmers with a great deal of freedom in terms of controlling the memory that has been allocated.

Even in the situation of automatically allocated material, it is impossible to work properly when many function calls are made on the same object. Since only memory management allocation may be used across many scenarios owing to allocating space from either the heap or free memory, which is a portion of memory specifically organized for these operations, only memory access allocation can be utilized across numerous situations.

For manual allocation of memory blocks from the heap, library procedures (from the std lib. h header file), including such malloc (), may be used, with the applications accessing these blocks via pointers returned by malloc (). When memory is no longer required or utilized, it is deallocated, allowing it to be utilized for other reasons in the future.

C is a high-level programming language with certain boundaries and rules for memory management. For example, the rules for modifying the size of an array. To fully comprehend virtualization, we must first comprehend what an array is in its most basic form.

Arrays are collections of things stored in successive memory regions and may be thought of as collections of objects. Consider the following scenario: an array has a length of 6 items. However, only 3 of those elements must be inserted into the array. Fundamentally, in this circumstance, the leftover indices are a wastage of RAM.

8.4: Static Memory Allocation

When static memory allocation is used, the allocated memory is fixed and cannot be altered or altered after being allocated. Memory necessities must be determined before memory allocation to achieve better memory management.

For illustration, the array declares there is an instance of a static computer memory since the size of the collection must be known before it can be used in the program. Once the memory has been allocated, it is impossible to adjust the array's length.

```
#include<stdio.h>

void main()

{

int x[35], i;

for(i=0;i<35;i++){

cin>>x[i];

}

for(i=0;i<35;i++){

cout<<x[i];

}

}
```

The array's declaration is stable, and storage is allocated at the moment of building itself. Because the array's size is fixed, as proven by the value of int x[35], this illustrates static memory allocation. At any point throughout the program's execution, you will be unable to adjust the shape of the array.

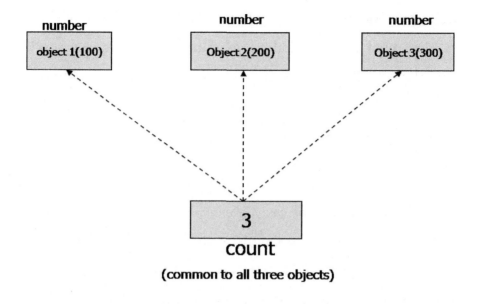

(common to all three objects)

8.5: Memory Allocation Prefixes

MALLOC:

Basic memory allocation is denoted by the prefix malloc in C, and its associated malloc () function is responsible for dynamically creating single big blocks of memory with a given size. This method returns pointers of the void type, which means that it has no effect.

They may now be manipulated and converted into references of any quantity or form, and the blocks are all initially initialized with default trash values as a result of the transformation. If there is inadequate space in the storage, the allocation operation will fail, and a NULL pointer will be returned.

Because it contains garbage values and if it is unable to allocate needed memory, this method revenues a null pointer when it is called. This algorithm allocates the memory during execution, but it does not initialize the memory allocation throughout execution.

Syntax:

While the amount of the cast-type or int (as seen in the example below) defines the byte length of the allocated memory, the pointer, which records the addresses of the initial bytes in the memory space, is affected by the size of a cast-type.

ptr = (castType*) malloc(size);

Code:

ptr = (float*) malloc(100 * sizeof(float));

CALL:

The term "cell" refers to "contiguous allocation," and the method malloc () is used to dynamically create many blocks of memory in the order specified by the arguments. Using calloc () is similar to using malloc (), with the distinction that malloc() initialized every block with the default value of zero, while calloc () initialized every block with the default value of void. The calloc () method may accept up to two inputs, referred to as parameters in the Python programming language.

(CastType*) calloc(n, size)

FREE:

The free () method is used to deallocate memory that has been allocated dynamically using the malloc () and calloc () functions (). Because just using free () is inadequate for deallocation, the library also includes the following extra methods. This function is essentially utilized for freeing up memory and, as a result, for minimizing the amount of space that is being used inefficiently.

If the memory space is not being used, it should be cleared or released. As mentioned above, in addressing, malloc () and calloc () functions only create a memory; they are unable to clear the memory on their own; thus, the free () method must be used directly to free the memory that is not currently in use to prevent memory leaks.

Syntax:

free(ptr_variable);

Malloc () and Free () together as follows:

#include <stdio.h>

#include <stdlib.h>

int main() {

```c
int n, i, *ptr, sum = 0;

printf("Enter the number of elements: ");
scanf("%d", &n);

ptr = (int*) malloc(n * sizeof(int));

// if memory cannot be allocated
if(ptr == NULL) {
  printf("Error! memory can not be allocated.");
  exit(0);
}

printf("Enter elements: ");
for(i = 0; i < n; ++i) {
  scanf("%d", ptr + i);
  sum += *(ptr + i);
}
```

```
printf("Sum = %d", sum);


// deallocating the memory

free(ptr);
}
```

Output:

Enter the number of elements: 3

Enter elements: 100

20

36

Sum = 156

REALLOC:

For example, suppose a user wishes to allocate additional memory, implying more than the program has started or requires. In that case, we may use the realloc () method to change the amount of memory that has already been allocated. Just as the name says realloc () enables memory to retain the previously specified values while allowing new memory regions to be allocated with garbage values. Similarly, if there is insufficient memory space, the allocation procedures will fail and produce NULL pointers.

Syntax:

```
ptr = realloc(ptr, x);
```

Code:

```c
#include <stdio.h>

#include <stdlib.h>


int main() {
  int *ptr, i , n1, n2;
  printf("Enter size of Memory: ");
  scanf("%d", &n1);


  ptr = (int*) malloc(n1 * sizeof(int));


  printf("Addresses of previous memory:\n");
  for(i = 0; i < n1; ++i)
    printf("%pc\n",ptr + i);


  printf("\nEnter the new size: ");
  scanf("%d", &n2);
```

```c
// reallocating the memory

ptr = realloc(ptr, n2 * sizeof(int));


printf("Addresses of new memory:\n");
for(i = 0; i < n2; ++i)
  printf("%pc\n", ptr + i);
free(ptr);
}
```

Output:

Enter size: 2

Addresses of previous memory:

26855472

26855476

Enter the new size: 4

Addresses of new memory:

26855472

26855476

8.6: Summary

Memory allocation is straightforward. It has two types of memory allocation: static memory allocation, which disburses memory all through compile-time or, in other words, before the program execution, and dynamic memory allocation, which assigns memory all through program execution or distributes memory during the program execution, and it makes use of four different functions: malloc (), malloc (), free (), and realloc (). Both approaches have advantages and disadvantages that are distinct from one another.

Chapter 9: Defining Keywords in C

9.1: Define the scope

Having just one key if you reside in an apartment complex is possible. This key will provide you with entry to your flat. Furthermore, the unit investor may have a key code that permits entry to all of the flats in the building.

```
                       int global;              // a global variable
                       int main()
                       {
                           int  local;          // a local variable

                           global = 1;          // global can be used here
                           local = 2;           // so can local

Scope of                   {                    // beginning a new block
global     Scope of            int  very_local  // this is local to the block
           local
                 Scope of          very_local = global+local;
                 very_local    }

                           // We just closed the block
                           // very_local can not be used
                       }
```

In C, variables are treated comparably to variables in other programming languages. The access of a variable inside a certain program or function is referred to as its variable scope. When it comes to C programming, a variable may be accessible just inside a certain function (for example, your home key), or it may be open to the whole program (for example, your apartment key) (the shared access key). The main function declaration and the main function declaration. In a C program, a variable may be declared in one of three places

- Outside of all functions, there is nothing (including the main). Global variables are the name given to this sort of variable.

- Inside the scope of a function or within a code section, Local variables are used to describe this sort of variable.

- In a function definition, this is denoted by the term formal parameter. This is analogous to a pointer defined inside the scope of a function's body.

The area of a program where the program may be referred to is the range of variables in the C programming language. Example: When we create a local object in a unit, it can only be referenced once it has been declared in that block, and it cannot be referenced in any other blocks nested inside that block. Block range and file scope are the two types of identifier scopes.

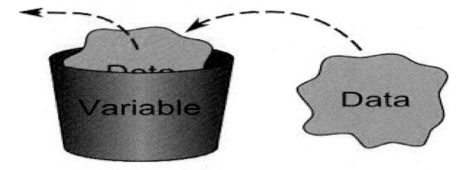

When it comes to computer programming, context is defined as delivering a term inside a program. In other words, the scope is the area of a script in which a constant is accessible for usage.

There are four different kinds of scopes:

- The file's scope

- The Block scopes

- The scope of the function

- The scope of the prototype

Because they are exclusively functional in that particular apartment, we may compare the apartment codes to operands in a programming language. A function's variables (keys) are unique to that function. The term "global variables" refers to factors (keys) that are accessible across the whole program (apartment building).

A scope is an area to which a variable has access in any programming language. The global key will not function outside of the apartment building, and the key for room 237 will only function inside the apartment complex's confines. Let's look at how this is implemented in the C programming language.

```
#include <stdio.h>

int global = 5;

void display()

{
```

```c
    printf("%d\n", global);
}
int main()
{
    printf("Before changing within main: ");
    display();

    printf("After changing within main: ");
    global = 10;
    display();
}
```

Output:

Before changing within main: 5

After changing within main: 10

9.2: Define Visibility

The accessibility of a statistic is described as whether a variable is available or not inside a certain piece of code or across the whole program.

The accessibility of a variable inside a system determines whether or not a variable is visible. A constant is visible when inside its context and hidden when outside its scope. The Conspicuousness of a variable determines how much of the entire program can access it. Depending on the situation, you may restrict the accessibility of a constant to a particular portion of a code, a specific feature, a specific source file, or any other location in a C program.

Storage Class	Keyword	Lifetime	Visibility	Initial Value
Automatic	auto	Function Block	Local	Garbage
External	extern	Whole Program	Global	Zero
Static	static	Whole Program	Local	Zero
Register	register	Function Block	Local	Garbage
Mutable	mutable	Class	Local	Garbage

The terms "visibility" and "scope" of a variable are quite similar; however, in a C program, every possible variable (within the scope) is not always visible (accessible). In this case, let us consider two variables with the same name, both of which are declared in two different scopes: one is available in the frame with the larger scope, but it is not usable because the variable proclaimed in the smaller scope has a greater priority in obtaining the variable asserted in the various inner block of code, and the other is an unavailable program to illustrate that a property is not visible even if it is declared in a block of code

#include stdio. #has a header file

main() #is a function that returns a value of type int.

int scope # variable in the outer scope

10 #is the scope of the project.

#This is the code contained inside the inner block of code.

{

the float scope; and the inner scope

2.98 is the breadth of the problem.

printf("Inner block scope: percent fn", scope); printf("Inner block scope: percent fn", scope);

}

printf("Outer block scope: percent dn", scope); printf("Outer block scope: percent dn", scope);

return the value 0;

}

9.3: Define Extent

The lifespan of a statistic or function is measured in terms of the time it takes to allocate memory to store it and the time it takes to free up the memory that was allocated. The laws of Extent and nature impact the method functions and data operations, and they are essential in the design of C-based applications.

The laws of scope impact how objects and data communicate, and they are important in designing C-based applications. This chapter investigates the different storage types responsible for controlling these attributes. The focus is on how scope and Extent control make it easier to write modular programs and, specifically, how it makes it easier to build multiple-file applications.

A function with the parameters int a and integer b is called a function (int a, int b). statements {int val2 = 5; int val3 = 5; statements. In this case, val2 is considered out of scope. statements

* The variables a, b, and Val are no longer relevant here *

Extern is a keyword in the C program writing language used to define a global variable, which is a variable that does not have any memory associated with it. In header files, it is used to define variables and functions, among other things. Extern is a function that can access variables across several C files.

9.4: Define Linkage

The word "identifier" is used in C, but the term "name" is used (both of which are what C++ adopts to formalize Linkage). A procedure known as Linkage may be used to make an identifier that has been declared in many contexts or even in the same scope multiple times, corresponding to almost the same product or function.

The relationship between a name and its scope is linked to, but separate from, its scope. The area of a language pair where a name is visible is referred to as the scope of the name. If a name has a wide range (the same as a document in C and the same as a global namespace scope in C++), it is visible across the whole file. Whether or not that term has been granted external or internal connection, its scope will stop after the translation unit.

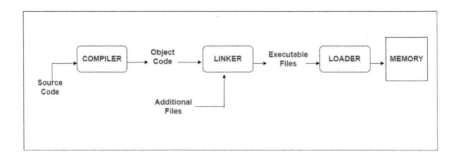

The name's entity may be referenced from another language pair using a distinct statement for that same name and from multiple scopes within the same language pair using separate declarations if that name has external Linkage. If the name were to be given an internal connection, such a declaration would represent a separate entity, even though it is using the same name, yet its entity might be referred to by different declarations inside the same translation unit if the name were to be given internal Linkage. Using a name that has no connection to anything else means that it cannot be referenced from statements in different scopes, or even from declarations within the same subchannel. Parameters of procedures and local variables are two examples of such designations. THERE ARE DIFFERENCES IN THE SPECIFICS between C (in which only objects and functions, not types, are linked) and C++ and this simplified summary.

When linking languages, a prodigious deal of care must be taken since various languages embellish their outward symbols differently. When linking C++ and C code, a frequent approach is to use the extern "C" keyword.

9.5: Define Block scope of variables:

A block is a collection of statements in computer programming surrounded by the left and right guards, respectively. The C block, a frame that may have other blocks inside it, is where blocks may be nested. If you define a variable in a block, it is available inside the block and any inner sections of that component, but it is not usable outside the block itself.

#Includestdio.h #is a header file

int main ()

{

integers a = 10 and b = 20;

printf("a = percent d, b = percent dn", a, b);

integer b is equal to 30;

printf("a = percent d, b = percent dn", a, b); printf("a = percent d, b = percent dn", a, b);

printf("a = percent d, b = percent dn", a, b); printf("a = percent d, b = percent dn", a, b);

}

Variables a and b are defined and initialized with the values 10 and 20, respectively, at line number 5. Later on, a nested block is formed that prints the values of the variables. Because this is an inner block, elements a and b are available. The variable b is defined and initialized with the quantity 30 at the beginning of line 9. As a result, the outer variable 'a' will be increased by one, making a=10+1=11. However, the next line, b++, raises the internal variable b by one, making b = 30+1=31. The printf function is used to show these data. Later in the program, the constant inner b is likewise released from memory allocation after the inner loop is made. As a result, the values of the outer elements a and b are printed in the final printf command.

```
#include <stdio.h>

int main()

{

int my_num = 7;

{

    //add 10 my_num

    my_num = my_num +10;

    //or my_num +=10 - more succinctly

    printf("my_num is %d",my_num);

}

    return 0;
```

}

In C, a part of the code is delimited by the symbol. The curly brackets at the beginning and end of a block denote the beginning and completion of a block, respectively, in the code. Throughout the outer block, the integer variable my num is initialized to the value 7; This variable is used by the main () method. There is an internal block that attempts to increase the value of the variable my num by 10.

```c
int main()

{

    int my_num = 7;

    {

        int new_num = 10;

    }

    printf("new_num is %d",new_num); //this is line 9

    return 0;

}
```

This program's main () function has a variable named my num, located in the outer block. The inner block also contains the initialization of another variable, new num. This means that the outer block is nestled inside the wider block.

In the outer block, we're attempting to access and output the value of the new num variable from the inner block. The range of a variable determines the portions of a program from which other sections may access a variable. The situation in which a variable is defined determines the variable's scope.

Chapter: 10 Working with Files

When interacting with files, you must specify a connection of type file to do the job. This declaration is required for the file and the application to communicate with one another.

10.1 Opening and reading text file

We use the open () function previously discussed to create or open a file. It should go without mentioning that the first is the most important. The step-in file handling is creating or opening a file. Having created the file, it may be accessed, updated, or removed throughout its existence.

The fundamental syntax for opening a file is as follows:

The function FILE *open(const char *filename, const char *mode) returns the reference to the file. This reference to the file is what creates the link between the file and the application; it is referred to as the *pointer variable. *filename is the file's name in this case. * The method we operate is referred to as opening our document.

The following are the several ways in which the file may be opened:

- **Rb:** It is used to open a binary code in reading mode, which we want.

- **Wb:** This program is used to open or generate a binary file in writing mode.

- **Ab:** It is used to access a binary file in attach mode, which is convenient.

- **rb+:** When we open a binary file, we may do it in neither reading nor writing mode.

- **wb+:** We may do it in both reading modes when opening a binary file.

- **ab+:** We may do it in both learnings to read mode when opening a binary file.

Consider the scenario in which the file newprogram.txt does not exist in the directory E: programs. The first function generates a new file called newprogram.txt and opens it for editing in the mode 'w.' The second function establishes a different document called newprogram.txt and publishes it for writing in the mode 'w.'

The writing mode enables you to create and change (overwrite) the file's text while still in editing mode. We will assume that the second code file old program existed in the directory E: programs for argument. The second code opens the executable program in byte mode 'RB' for reading purposes, whereas the first function does the opposite. The reading mode enables you to simply read from the file; it does not allow you to write to the file.

Writing to a text file in C language as follows

```c
#include <stdio.h>

#include <stdlib.h>

int main()

{

    int num;

    FILE *fptr;

    fptr = fopen("C:\\program.txt","w");

    if(fptr == NULL)

    {

        printf("Error!");

        exit(1);

    }


    printf("Enter num: ");

    scanf("%d",&num);
```

```c
    fprintf(fptr,"%d",num);

    fclose(fptr);


    return 0;
}
```

Read a text file in C language as follows:

```c
#include <stdio.h>

#include <stdlib.h>

int main()

{

    int num;

    FILE *fptr;


    if ((fptr = fopen("C:\\program.txt","r")) == NULL){

        printf("Error! opening file");

        exit(1);

    }


    fscanf(fptr,"%d", &num);
```

```
printf("Value of n=%d", num);

fclose(fptr);

}
```

10.2 Using a for loop to read text files:

The file that will be created must exist in the same listing as the executable file for this application to be opened. First, we must open the file in any of the available modes. For example, if you merely want to read the file, you should open it in "r" mode. We are only permitted to conduct specific actions on the file depending on the chosen model during file opening. For instance, if you open the file in "r" mode, you will not be capable of writing to the file since "r" mode is a read-only method that only enables the reading of the file. During a read operation, the structure to which the file position indication points are read and written to the disc. After the structure has been read, the pointer is shifted to point to the next structure in the sequence. When reading from a document, I'm experiencing trouble, yet, the first printout outside of the cycle is completed successfully. However, nothing is taken from the file while the for loop runs.

- Create variables and the file pointer in Step 1 of the process.

- Using the file, go to Step 2.

- If the file cannot be opened, a notice indicating the problem is printed in Step 3.

- Using the loop, print the contents of the text file that was created before in Step 4

- Step 5 is to Save and close the file

10.3 Writing a text file

The following is a list of the three sorts of streams (sequences of bytes) that may be found in a file after we have discussed how to open and shut a file:

- Input

- Output

- Input/Output (I/O)

Using the input/output procedures in a file, you may read and write data into and out of a file. The simplest methods for conducting actions on words in files are () and put (), which are used to read and write characters in a file. Data collection in a file is read and written using Python's fscanf () and fprintf () expressions.

```
#include stdio.h>

#include stdlib.h>

#include stdlib.h

{

id number;

*fptr; FILE *fptr

if ( ptr is not NULL)

{

printf("Error!");

exit(1);

}

printf("Enter the following number: ");

scanf(" percent d",&num); scanf(" percent d",&num)

"percent d",num; fprintf(fptr," percent d",num);

fclose(fptr);

return the value 0;


}
```

Program.txt is a text file that contains the results of the user's selection of a random number.

10.4 Opening and reading text files by the buffer size

You may read binary information from a file line and place it in an integer or other chunk of memory while programming in the Program code. The main program function read () can be used to accomplish this task. This function is accessible in most C implementations that provide access to the control system's file system, including the C programming language. Read () can read from hardware devices (especially character-based devices) on GNU/Linux versions of windows that have device drivers associated with the file system.

You must first open a file to be able to read from it. Furthermore, after working with the folder, you should shut it to enable other apps to access the data. The two functions that you will be using are open () and close () (). Although the emphasis of this lecture is on fread () and not on basic file-handling procedures, a quick overview of these routines may be beneficial. Open () accesses a file for learning to write and returns a reference to a stream of data from the opened file. Two cases specify a file to be created: the primary work (which may or may not include a path) and the next is the accessing mode, which may be one of seven matches. This example code opens a file for reading, which uses the access mode "r" to do just that. When using this parameter, the file must already be present.

Close () shuts the file and removes any locks held by it. This function accepts only one parameter: the pointer provided by a valid call to open ().

```
int main( int argc, const char* argv[] )

{

    FILE *rm;

    char buf[201];

    printf("\r\nUdemy.com - Reading from Files in C\r\n");

    rm = fopen("ReadMe.txt", "r");
```

```c
if (rm != NULL) {

    fread(buf, 1, 200, rm);

    buf[(sizeof buf)-1] = 0;

    printf("%s", buf);

    fclose(rm);

}

    else

        printf("File Not Found.\r\n");

}

size_t fread(void *ptr, size_t size, size_t nmemb, FILE *stream);
```

10.5 Opening, reading, and writing binary files

Reading and writing data from a binary file are accomplished using the () and write() functions. When compared to dealing with text files, binary files are a little harder to work with since the syntax requires the usage of extra parameters. The functions read () and write () need four parameters to operate properly.

The following is the fundamental syntax for accessing a binary file in C:

The function () reads the data from the specified address, size, number of data items, and file pointer.

The following is the fundamental syntax for writing to a binary file in C:

File writing is done using the function write (data address, size of data, number of data items, file pointer). It is necessary to utilize the write () method to write into a binary file. The functions require the following two arguments:

- Address of the data that will be written to the disc

- Amount of data that will be written to disc

10.6 Deleting and renaming files

The remove () method is responsible for removing a file from storage. For example, the function remove ("myfile.dat") removes the file myfile.dat from memory. The remove () function accepts a C-style string of any length as an argument. A string-type variable cannot be used as an argument; instead, you must use the.c str () function to convert them to a regular C++ string variable type.

#includestdio.h> //for the delete() and rename() functions ( )

#include "apstring.cpp" //as a dependency.

(void)

{

//fileToDelete apstring fileToDelete;

cout "Arrive the name of the file to be deleted:";

getline(cin,fileToDelete);

if (remove(fileToDelete.c str()) is not equal to zero)

removal operation failed endl; cout "Remove operation failed."

else

"coutfileToDelete" has been deleted from the program." endl;

return the value 0;

}

The rename () method accepts the name of a folder and the new title of the file, with the second parameter being the new title of the file. In the following example, the function renames ("myfile.dat," "newfile.dat") and renames the file myfile.dat to newfile.dat. In addition, the rename () method takes string parameters in the C manner.

If the file indicated by newname existed, it was destroyed. If the new and old names are not in the same domain, it is equal to transferring the file.

Rename directory:

If both the old name and old name are folders, rename the directory. If the directory provided by the newname exists and is vacant, the new name is first erased. The caller process must have written rights for new and old name directories. When you rename a file, the new name cannot have the old name as its path beginning. For example, you cannot change /use to /use/foo/test directory since the old name (/use/foo) is a path precursor to the new name and cannot be deleted.

Conclusion

C is a robust general-purpose programming language that can be used for an assortment of tasks. It may be used to create software such as databases, operating systems, compilers, and other similar applications. C programming is an ideal language for beginners to learn to program since it is simple and straightforward.

Due to its reputation as "the mother of all programming languages," the C programming language has gained widespread popularity. Memory management is quite versatile in this language due to its flexibility. C is the most suitable programming language for system-level programming.

This book covers a broad scale of subjects, starting with the most basic issues, such as "What is C?" and moving through the usage of complicated C tools, such as pointers, functions, and dealing with files, to the most advanced topics, such as object-oriented programming. Therefore, both beginner readers and advanced readers will benefit from it.

Additionally, by reviewing the examples offered in each chapter and area of the book, one may assess their comprehension of a certain topic. The book includes a summary of functions, data types, and problem-solving approaches to make it easier to study the material.

Aside from that, this book is divided into two sections: the first half will teach you the fundamentals of C programming, including variable initialization, data types, conditional statements, functions, and pointers; the second half will teach you advanced C programming notions, such as preprocessors, memory manipulation, defining scope, and working with files; and the final half will teach you how to write C programs that run on multiple computers. File Handling is covered in detail in a separate module that teaches how to use C programs to create and update files stored on the local file system and how to read and remove files from the file system.

The second portion will cover the fundamentals of file management, such as creating, reading, deleting, and updating files. The concept of Memory Manipulation will be explained in the second segment as well. It also contains a separate Memory Manipulation module that discusses the importance of memory and how to use and control it in C programs.

This book on the principles of C programming is just the start of a journey that will lead to the development of a programmer's talents. The fact that you were able to solve all of the examples provided suggests that you have earned a significant amount of knowledge and competence in the core programming ideas that are used in conjunction with the C programming language. Presume you are involved in learning more about programming. In that case, you are about to start an in-depth study of the subject in which you will enhance your software development abilities and gain technical knowledge about the C programming language.

Printed in Great Britain
by Amazon

20684210R00147